You've been lied to.

They told you to get the degree. Build the business.
Climb the ladder. Play nice. Stay balanced. Keep going.
Smile for the photos. Post the wins. Be grateful.

And now, here you are—successful, exhausted,
half-alive, pretending.

You don't need another routine. You don't need more tools.
You don't need more f*cking balance.

You need truth. You need clarity.
You need your fire back.

I wrote this book for the high performers who feel lost.

For those who checked all the boxes
and still feel like something's off.

For the people who are done playing the game
by the system's rules.

This is not a self-help book.
It's a wake-up call. A gut-punch. A fire-starter.
A mirror.

It's not about fixing your life.

It's about finally seeing it for what it is—and having the
balls (or the courage) to do something about it.

So take a breath.

And whatever you do...

...don't fog it up.

Praise for *UNfogged*

"This book opened my eyes. Thank you, Constantin."

MARY W.

"There are books that you put away without a thought. This one became my companion. I take it everywhere; It's an inspiration."

CAYTLIN H.

"When I thought I'd hit rock bottom, I found this book and the Dietrich Institute: My life saver."

KEN S.

"A story of courage and the essence of what really counts... about how quickly things can go bad. It changed my perspective."

GEORGE K.

"I bought it because I liked the title. And then I really liked the message. Great book."

JUAN C.

UNFOGGED

UNFOGGED

Seven Secrets to True Clarity,
True Connections, and
True Success

CONSTANTIN DIETRICH

GRAMMAR
FACTORY
— EST? 2013 —

Published by Grammar Factory Publishing,
an imprint of MacMillan Company Limited.

Grammar Factory Publishing
MacMillan Company Limited
25 Telegram Mews, 39th Floor, Suite 3906
Toronto, Ontario, Canada
M5V 3Z1

www.grammarfactory.com

Dietrich, Constantin
UNfogged: Seven Secrets to True Clarity, True Connections, and True Success.

Paperback ISBN 978-1-998756-59-9
Hardcover ISBN 978-1-998756-61-2
eBook ISBN 978-1-998756-60-5
Audiobook ISBN 978-1-998756-62-9

1. FAM029000 FAMILY & RELATIONSHIPS /
Love & Romance. 2. FAM030000 FAMILY & RELATIONSHIPS /
Marriage & Long-Term Relationships. 3. BUS107000 BUSINESS &
ECONOMICS / Personal Success.

Production Credits

Interior layout design by Setareh Ashrafologhalai
Book production and editorial services by Grammar Factory Publishing

Grammar Factory's Carbon Neutral Publishing Commitment

Grammar Factory Publishing is proud to be neutralizing the carbon footprint of all printed copies of its authors' books printed by or ordered directly through Grammar Factory or its affiliated companies through the purchase of Gold Standard-Certified International Offsets.

Disclaimer

To my mother:
A pillar of grace and unyielding strength.
Though your presence is now beyond this world,
your spirit lives on—in me, in my family, in all that we
are and all that we strive to become.
We are your legacy, not only through blood but through
the sacrifices you made and the unshakable foundation
you built with love, faith, and tireless devotion.

This is for you and for all who bear the weight of love's
greatest calling: to nurture, to sacrifice, and to create a
better future for their children.

CONTENTS

FOREWORD
BY KIKI KUHNERT

P EOPLE WHO DO what they say are my favorite kind of people, and Tino is such a person. He transformed personal disaster into wonderful energy, channeling it to a whole new form of support.

Unfogged.

We've all experienced that beautiful moment when the fog begins to clear in the morning. It's as if the veil of uncertainty has been lifted. From the moment I first read the title of this book, I loved it. It says so much. Also, about Tino.

Tino has helped countless couples and individuals to create the life of their dreams. His interest in each individual is sincere and honest and his love for his wife and children is wonderful. Seeing them together makes you think: "I want to live like them."

As both a friend and a colleague, I know that getting to where they are was not always easy. Commitment, dedication, understanding, clarity and love... and the willingness to hold onto the treasures they have, has allowed Tino and his wonderful wife to preserve their marriage and family.

And so, Tino's approach to helping his clients is a great combination of knowledge, empathy, self-experience and a love for people.

He is a person you really must get to know. Congratulations... you start doing so by reading this book. And who knows; perhaps we will meet each other one day at the Dietrich Institute.

KIKI KUHNERT

Entrepreneur, passionate life coach, internationally recognized author, award-winning philanthropist and mother

PREFACE
THIS CAN'T BE IT

T HE PHONE RANG, as shrill as the alarms that often pierced the air. In a hospital bed at the Baptist Hospital Intensive Care Unit in Miami in early summer 2020, a man pushed away the stiff white sheets that entombed him and picked up the receiver a nurse was offering him. He could barely draw breath—his chest was tight, and each intake of air lanced him with pain.

It was all he could do to rasp out a greeting. "Hello?"

He aimed the phone away from his mouth, as if he might somehow spread the virus to the caller, and coughed, the sound harsh and rattling.

"Good afternoon," said a calm voice on the other end of the line. "I'm the reverend of Pastoral Care.

We're calling to ask whom you would like for us to contact in case of an emergency."

The patient was heavily medicated, though no amount of painkillers could remove the ache in his chest. He found himself struggling to make sense of the caller's words.

After a moment, he got there. "My wife."

He had messaged his wife when he entered this place, saying he thought they wanted to keep him there for a night or so. At least, that was the last message he remembered sending.

"What is your religion?" the caller asked gently.

Confused, the man told him he was Christian.

"Do you have a last will?" the reverend continued. "Any special wishes?"

At first, the man didn't understand what he was being asked. *Why is he asking me these questions? Is it some kind of admissions protocol?*

Then, he had a glimmer of understanding. *Oh. He's probably calling to see if I want to attend Sunday Mass or something.*

But even as that thought occurred to him, he became aware of the machines beeping next to him, an incessant rhythm that you didn't want to falter. Two medical staff—nurses, he presumed—rushed past the door, indistinguishable from one another in their white hazmat suits, a familiar rustling accompanying their hurried steps. And then he realized he was being asked whether he had plans in place if he didn't make it out of this ICU. If he died.

He glanced at the contraption beside him, which took up almost as much space as his bed, connected to his insides by crimson-filled tubes attached via intravenous cannulas whose sharp pinch he could feel every time he moved a fraction. It was an ECMO machine, something that took his blood entirely out of his body, bypassing his heart and lungs, oxygenating it before returning it to his system via his jugular. It was keeping him alive. But who knew for how long?

"Would you like for me to pray for you?" the reverend went on, even more gently.

"Uh, yes," the man said, squeezing his eyes shut and feeling perversely glad, for a passing moment, that he was allowed no visitors on this ward, so his family—his wife, his children, his parents—could not see how close to breaking he was. "Yes, I would."

"Lord," the reverend began, "please welcome this man with open arms..."

Now the man understood the call. Now he understood everything. This was his last prayer.

Tears sprang to his eyes. He tried to concentrate on the reverend's words. He tried to join in with the prayer.

The reverend finished. The call ended. The nurse standing beside him took the receiver and put the phone down. The patient looked at her, struggling to take a breath.

"I'll be okay, right?" he asked.

The nurse just looked at him. She was not allowed to make him any promises. She couldn't have said yes, even if she did have any confidence that he would get out of here.

"We don't know," she said quietly. "But we do everything we can."

She walked away and left the man crying into his pillow.

This can't be it, he thought. *It can't.*

IT WASN'T. That man was me, and I'm still here.

I began writing this book in spring of 2020, during the early weeks of the pandemic. But then my family members—all except my oldest son, Corbinian—were all diagnosed with Covid-19. So I had to re-prioritize. As it was for so many of us, my plans were postponed by what 2020 had in store.

When I entered the ICU I'd already had Covid for over a month, and they hadn't yet realized that it wasn't just my lungs that were affected. Months later, a cardiologist made a distressing discovery: he told me that I'd acquired a heart infection, which had left scar tissue on that vital organ. Treatment involved entering a hyperbaric (or altitude) chamber to help my body come to terms and learn to live with a lack of oxygen.

A few short years ago (at the time of writing), we were all confronted with Covid. My story might sound extreme—and I know how lucky I am to have survived—but we were all left with scars.

Do you remember being locked down in your home? We were desperate to go out and do things again, and we promised we would do those things differently. We wouldn't take anything—nor anyone—for granted, ever again. We said, "What would I give just to go out for dinner? To travel, to see my family, my friends, to get back in the gym, the pool, the park? To visit an art gallery, an exhibition, a market? To go to a show, listen to live music, perform for a crowd? To enter even a supermarket without wearing a mask?"

Many people asked themselves, "How am I ever going to meet someone now?" Even once lockdown was lifted, if you wanted to date, you did it in a mask.

People suffered from illness, and they suffered from frustration. They suffered the loss of loved ones and the loss of their freedom. Many of us suffered from loneliness.

When I enter a restaurant now (which, for a long while, was an impossibility), I often think, how is it we're back sitting at tables with our friends and family, but also back just staring at our phones? Why aren't we engaging with each other with all the fervor that comes from having experienced our social life being taken away? Today we are free, but instead of taking what happened to us all as a chance to embrace change and truly enjoy one another, we're back to our previous habits. We've forgotten that we once asked that question: "What would I give?"

Fortunately, the rest of my family was spared from serious illness. But Covid really hit me hard. While I lay in my bed in the Baptist Hospital ICU, every labored breath reminded me of how serious my situation had become, and how precious each moment of life is.

In the midst of our bustling lives, amid the cacophony of our routines, we often forget the simple joys—the tiny moments that give life its true essence. Isn't it ironic? If we wake up with the flu, we curse the inconvenience it brings, yet how many times have we woken up just grateful for the absence of it? We have a knack for taking everyday miracles for granted. But with Covid, life, in its unpredictable way, gave us a stark reminder of how precious it is.

As I sat there in hospital, sifting through the countless messages—all these different voices and opinions—it was as though I was wearing glasses with lenses fogged by steam. Everything was blurred, and clarity seemed like a distant dream. Amidst the chaos, however, I came to a profound realization. We're given this exquisite gift called life, an unpredictable journey with no guarantee of tomorrow. Just as suddenly as we're thrust onto this beautiful planet, in a blink, we could be taken away. The Latin phrase "carpe diem" began resonating deeply inside me, urging me to seize the day, the moment, the now.

Life's unpredictability has taught me to live with intention, to find purpose, to seek clarity, and, above all, to cherish every moment. To not just breathe, but truly live; to not just exist, but thrive; to not just hear, but listen; to not just look, but truly see. And it's this revelation that has pushed me to share my journey, my insights, my hopes, and my visions with others.

In my hometown of Hamburg, a port city in the northern part of Germany, where stories thrive behind every door, there's a man called Folker Henschel. With scissors in one hand and decades of wisdom in the other, he's been my barber and personal sage for over thirty years. Through the intimacy of whispered tales, punctuated by the clip of freshly cut hair, Folker, a shining example of happiness and profound simplicity, has taught me more about life than a hundred big books. Each time we meet, I'm reminded that, sometimes, the most enlightening conversations happen not in libraries or lecture halls, but right there in the stylist's chair. Folker isn't just a hairdresser—he's one of Hamburg's unsung philosophers.

In a world where tomorrow isn't promised, it's essential to make every moment count. And as my good friend Folker has mused, "In the end, isn't life about finding the kind of love and purpose that fills not just our homes, but our very souls?" So, here's to living a life of clarity, consciousness, and, above all, compassion.

Covid has given us the opportunity to appreciate what's important. We need to embrace the options that we're given in life, so we can help people where we can and share our knowledge where it's needed. In a world and in relationships that have somehow become so fogged up, we can choose to clear the air—to wipe those lenses clean.

As soon as I recovered, I determined to put my energy toward these kinds of meaningful pursuits. And that's why I've written this book.

INTRODUCTION
7 BEACONS TO IGNITE
A BLISSFUL LIFE

THE MELLOW NOTES of Sinatra's "That's Life" welcome me into Bar Bleu and Hamburg's Hotel Tortue. As I settle into a plush seat, the ambiance whisks me back to my first-ever visit there, on September 25th, 2018. It was a memorable evening orchestrated by Claus, a lifelong friend I'd known since our kindergarten days. Alongside him was Anina, his ever-devoted wife, and two of our cherished friends from Hamburg.

Ever since I moved to Miami, my trips to Hamburg aren't merely visits, but heartfelt reunions—opportunities to catch up, relive old memories, and create new ones. It is now October 2021. Tonight, I am meeting with my dear friend Tommy, and it is poised to be another of those nights. However, the deafening silence of Claus's absence is palpable. Losing him to Covid in early 2020 has left an irreplaceable void in many hearts, most profoundly in those of Anina and their two boys. Claus and Tommy shared the role of godfather to my daughter, Calyssa, which bound our hearts even closer. Now, the two of us who remain sit in Bar Bleu, grieving his loss.

Tommy notices my gaze and nudges me gently. "Claus was one of a kind," he murmurs, his voice soft with shared pain.

I nod, lost momentarily in memories of a friend who journeyed with me through so many of life's highs and lows.

"He truly was. He and Anina had that rare kind of bond," I reply.

In the midst of this melancholy nostalgia, the waitress approaches, balancing her tray of glittering glasses. She sets down our drinks with practiced ease, and her face softens with a kind smile. "Diving into the past tonight?"

Tommy, a mischievous glint in his eyes, remarks, "With Tino? Always. Life's been quite the ride, hasn't it?"

Grinning despite the pangs of remembrance, I set my notepad on the table. "Every story has its chapters. That's why I'm writing this book."

Tommy grins. "And that's why I want to hear all about it."

We have met here so that I can take him through the tapestry of memories, experiences, and lessons that I lay out in these pages for you to read—to lead him through the plan, chapter by chapter, and explain what I want you, the reader, to take away from it all. It's a road map for what to expect from the journey.

"There are seven beacons of clarity," I tell him. "When I almost died, I spent so much time connecting the dots and going over—reliving—the events of my life, coming to understand what everything was there to teach me. Nothing happened *to* me—it all happened *for* me. And now I understand the lessons that life, the universe, has kept trying to present me with, sometimes over and over again without me listening! Now I've looked back and realized what it was always trying to tell me—and it all comes down to these seven beacons of awareness, which light a path through the fog. I've finally listened! And I'm ready to share, to help others understand how to get to clarity without needing a near-death experience first."

Tommy nods, encouraging me to go on. "So, what are these beacons? Where do we start?"

I give him the summary—the route the book will take.

"The first beacon is self-awareness. Everything starts with where you've come from, who raised you, what you've been through—this is what shapes you and your beliefs, your values, without you even realizing it at the time."

"That makes sense," Tommy says. "So, you'll speak about your family?"

"Yes. My mother, my grandmother, the life of my grandfather... it's obvious to me now what their influence has been on my life. How they—and others—have affected the choices I've made, which in turn have determined the challenges I've faced."

Tommy nods. "What was it your mother used to say to you?"

I take a deep breath. "'Be clear, believe, focus, and it shall be.' I've always held to that, and it's never let me down."

"I know there'll be some interesting tales there," Tommy says. "What comes next?"

"The next beacon is harmony. When I first started exploring being an entrepreneur—even as early as my school days—I threw myself into everything with such great ambition, but I never paused to think about what things meant. I wasn't truly present. And I fell into that trap of overworking and looking at life through the lens of having to choose to maintain a 'work-life balance,' which is a complete myth. Being in balance as a person is part of practicing conscious-ness—it's not this 'work is work and separate from life' bullshit."

Tommy frowns. "I've fallen into that trap myself. So, you'll talk about your first ventures into business?"

"Yes. And the lessons I learned from the friends I made while traveling to and working in Mexico and China, across Southeast Asia, as well as in Germany, Switzerland, Canada, and the States."

I grow silent for a moment, musing on those tran-sitions. "When I look back, I see I perpetually danced on the edge of now, with one foot anchored in tomor-row's 'what's next' and the other adrift in yesterday. Caught in a delicate balance reminiscent of yin and yang—the ancient Chinese philosophy of opposing, yet complementary forces—I came to understand that true harmony doesn't hinge on the extremes of past or future, but rather lies in immersing oneself entirely in the present moment."

I pause before concluding on this point. Grasping that there's a harmony to life is so important. "We should be looking at life as one harmonious whole—making choices that consciously serve this, rather than breaking it down into parts and placing them in opposition to each other. That's what makes you ill."

Tommy raises his hands. "For sure. Look at burn-out culture. Look at how sick we're making ourselves. I know Covid wasn't the first time you were seriously unwell."

I shrug. "What can I say? My body—my life—has offered me more than one wake-up call. But you have to be living consciously to hear those calls and act on them."

We pause, thinking on that for a beat. I know Tommy's had wake-up calls of his own.

"So what comes next?" he asks.

"The beacon of self-belief," I answer. "It's about your relationship with yourself—about holding true to your values and not letting others who aren't aligned with you lead you astray."

"Some people have put roadblocks in your way," Tommy says.

"Yes, and I didn't always make wise decisions. I had great ideas, and sometimes I walked away when maybe I should have done differently."

Tommy looks thoughtful. "You're talking about the energy-drink revolution. You were among the first to go there. That was a groundbreaking move, introducing energy drinks to the world."

I sip my drink and gaze into the past. "It was. And I learned about so much more than innovation and marketing. This beacon is about overcoming the challenges people put in front of you when they don't believe in you. To do that, you have to believe in yourself."

Tommy swirls the ice in his glass. "Where some people see dead ends, you build bridges."

I raise my hands. "Exactly! When I involved Vietnam in the United Nations' Oil for Food Program, there were so many hurdles to overcome—there was no shipping fleet to transport the rice, for a start! But if you believe in your dream, then you can manifest your vision. You just need the drive to do so. And to pick yourself up when you get knocked down."

Tommy grimaces, as though his drink's taste has turned sour. "Like by the dot-com crash."

"Sometimes the bubble bursts," I say, shaking my head at the memory. "It's what you do after that counts."

"So where does the book take us next?" Tommy asks.

"To the next beacon—compassion. There's a rhythm to be found in all our relationships. Not just with our romantic partners, our lovers, but with everyone."

Tommy laughs, interrupting me. "Well, with all the time you spent in the online dating industry, you'd know."

I grin. Not everyone takes the idea seriously, but some of the heaviest lessons I learned came from that time in the trenches of the online world with all those people looking for love—looking for something they were missing.

"It's not complicated," I say. "But compassion, empathy, kindness—nobility—they aren't just important to how we engage in our relationships with others. They are how we change the world, one act at a time."

Tommy sobers at the thought. "It was your research into relationships that really sowed the seeds for the Dietrich Institute, wasn't it?"

"Yes. Our relationships are the most important things in the world. They form us, and they are how we find happiness—in ourselves and in others. Getting clear on that is everything."

"So what comes after that?" Tommy asks.

"Perspective," I say. "This beacon is about looking through life's unfiltered lens and understanding key truths about the possibility of healing from old wounds and the so-called 'pursuit of happiness.' This is only possible through a shift in perspective. And one thing that shift will bring you is embodied in the next beacon."

"Which is?"

"Purpose. For me, that's the Dietrich Institute, and everything it stands for: Clarity, Consciousness, Compassion. Helping people heal themselves and their relationships and form loving homes, infused with family values."

The waitress has refilled our glasses, and I take a deep breath and a long drink. I need a moment to recall how long and how much it took for me to come to my purpose. Clarity around this is what has imbued my life with meaning.

Tommy nods gently. "Going into coaching was one of the best things you could have done."

I laugh, and we clink glasses. "It was! Building the institute was about designing a vehicle for my purpose, to help people not just in one aspect, but holistically, in their whole lives. Because our lives are a series... no, a web of relationships. How we perceive them, understand them, communicate within them... that is what controls how we flourish."

"It reminds me of that Harvard study on happiness you told me about,"[1] Tommy comments. "The longest study of its kind to be conducted?"

"Yes!" I exclaim. "That study examined what makes people happiest in life over an entire lifetime, what makes us thrive, and even live longer. It's not money..." We both laugh at that. "It's not eating well

---

1 Mineo, L. "Good genes are nice, but joy is better." *The Harvard Gazette*, April 2017. Accessed online 30 August 2023. https://news.harvard.edu/gazette/story/2017/04/over-nearly-80-years-harvard-study-has-been-showing-how-to-live-a-healthy-and-happy-life/

or exercising or advancing in our careers. It's positive relationships. All kinds of relationships! Our family, our friendships—at school, at work, in all the places we live and find community…" I clasp my hands together and lean across the table as though I'm telling Tommy some great secret. "Relationships are the key to happiness."

"How many beacons are there?" Tommy asks, counting off the ones I've told him about on his fingers.

"There are seven," I say, smiling. "And we're coming to the last one. Connection."

"What we're all looking for," Tommy comments.

I smile. He knows me well. This is why I wanted to speak to him about the book first.

"Exactly. Connection. Intimacy—emotional, not only physical. What are people after when they embark on an affair? What is everyone seeking, from their spouse, from their friends? It's understanding. It's trust. It's *listening*—communication. We are vulnerable creatures, and to feel safe, secure, loved, we need to share that vulnerability. We need to open up to and link up with others. That's what gives us peace."

I'm thinking about Claus again—he is never far from my thoughts. The connection we shared, the moments of vulnerability and deep joy.

Feeling a mixture of emotions, from melancholy to hope, I conclude, "This book is a tribute. To life, love, loss, and learning. A journey I invite every reader to share."

Tommy raises his drink in salute. "I can't wait to read it."

The ambiance of Bar Bleu holds us in a comforting embrace, offering us a cocktail of memories past and tales yet to be told.

WITH THIS book, I want to invite you to sit down with me and see how this has all come together—how it has all come to be. Perhaps you will recognize in my stories—my struggles and triumphs, all my learnings—stories of your own. And my hope is that, reflecting on your own experiences, you will see the seven beacons I've identified at work, and gain the clarity, consciousness, and compassion that has the power to change lives.

The 7 beacons

1. **Self-awareness**—the beacon of introspection, spotlighting our authentic self

2. **Harmony**—the beacon of balance, stopping us from veering too much in one direction

3. **Self-belief**—the beacon of our potential, ensuring we never forget our intrinsic worth

4. **Compassion**—the beacon of understanding, love, and kindness

5. **Perspective**—the beacon that acts as a vantage point, ensuring we don't get "lost in the moment" and can appreciate the grand tapestry of life

6. **Purpose**—the beacon that sheds light on our true calling, our *raison d'être* and true north

7. **Connection**—the beacon that weaves everything and everyone together, a reminder that our journey is intertwined with others

THE 7 BEACONS OF THE UNFOGGED LIFE

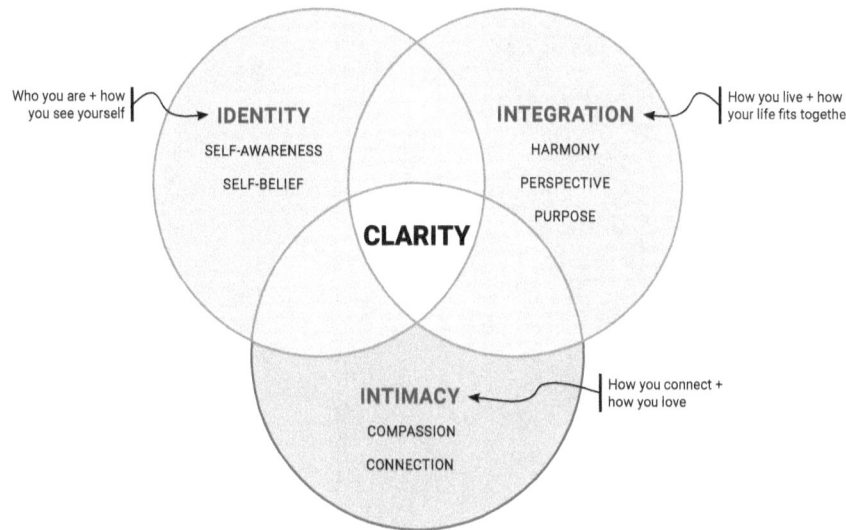

You don't find clarity. You align with it.

1

ROOTS OF
SELF-AWARENESS

I N THE VIBRANT tapestry of life, where threads of experience and memory intertwine, there are always those first stitches, the ones that ground us. Each of us is woven from stories, values, and beliefs whispered in our ears by those who came before us—our family.

From the bustling streets of my youth, the comforting scent of my grandmother's kitchen, and the strict discipline of a boarding school, I was handed down legacies, some written in bold letters while others were mere footnotes. Your first stitches were sewn for you, too. But what happens when we pause, remove those lenses that have been tinted with life's distractions, and truly examine these inherited tales? Do we carry them forward with us, cherishing them as heirlooms? Or do we come to the realization that some might be outdated hand-me-downs?

This chapter unpicks the threads of my own story—the echoes of resilience from a grandmother who faced unthinkable challenges, and the teachings of parents who were trying to craft a future for their child. It's a journey of discernment, of celebrating the inspirational and questioning received wisdom. Because I have come to realize that while we might be products of our past, the choice of what we carry forward is wholly ours.

As I unraveled the myriad tales of my upbringing, it became evident that our first beacon is self-awareness, a light in the fog that can help us understand who we are. It's not merely about recognizing the faces in old family photographs or remembering childhood stories—it's an acute understanding of where you come from, and a recognition of the imprints left on you by those tales and faces. It's about seeing the patterns, the passed-down beliefs, and the inherited values, some of which we might need to disavow. To truly grasp the significance of every whispered wisdom and every silent expectation, you need to gaze inward with a clear and discerning eye. To navigate the labyrinth of life and its countless choices, you must first understand the map etched within yourself.

This chapter is a guide to the sometimes-complicated root systems of self-awareness. It invites you to delve into your own narrative, to discern, to accept, and, most importantly, to choose.

THE SECRET OF
TRUE SELF-AWARENESS

When I lay in the ICU that summer of 2020, thinking I was about to die, I questioned my awareness and understanding of my identity. It was in that moment of vulnerability, amidst the beeping monitors and hushed conversations, that I found myself on an unexpected journey of self-reflection. I began to ponder the intricate forces that had shaped me throughout my life. Relationships, I realized, were the threads that had woven together the tapestry of my existence. From my bonds with family to the laughter shared with friends, the love of partners, camaraderie with colleagues, and my sense of belonging within my various global communities—these connections had defined me in profound ways. On top of this, coaching and mentoring had connected me with so many people, a testament to the interconnectedness of our common human experience.

Life has a way of throwing us unexpected curveballs, and it's in those pivotal moments that we're compelled to reflect and react. My moment had arrived in that ICU room—a stark reminder of life's fragility. It forced me to re-evaluate, to appreciate, and to recognize the profound importance of the relationships that define us.

In a way, everyone's story starts with their birth, and, therefore, their parents. We are more than the genes that have made us, but the people who have a hand in our creation and our upbringing are part of a puzzle, and you can only see the whole picture with clarity if you can examine the pieces and see how they've come together.

Tino and mother, 1973

How far we can come

I was born in Germany in October 1969. My parents split up before I came along, and I grew up with my mother in a small flat in Hamburg. My "bedroom" was the kitchenette, my bed a mattress squeezed into that tiny space, but I wasn't miserable. My dad married someone else and had other children, but he was part of my life. I had family who loved me, and my mom did everything in her power to make my childhood a happy one. She also showed me, in every word and action, how it's possible to make a success of yourself, no matter where you've come from, how your family circumstances are set, or what cards you've been dealt.

My mom started off selling curtains on the street. I remember well the garage in our apartment building where she stored them—we spent many Sundays in there, while she measured and cut fabric. Even though I was little, I did my best to help her pack the big bundles. When there were markets, she'd take her wares there, and me as well. I would wander all over, meeting the people at neighboring stalls who would turn up to all the same markets, all held in different places.

When my mother came to Hamburg in the early sixties, the Beatles were playing. She was originally from Berlin, but she had escaped in the late fifties before the Wall went up, arriving in Hamburg with only a few coins in her pocket. Once she got her trade license, she needed to innovate to get ahead. She dyed the originally yellowish curtain fabrics snow-white, which made her the first in Germany to offer this product in this color. This was an ingenious idea, and she was soon able to serve over fifty weekly markets from one stall, carrying a camp bed to sleep on.

Mother's garage in Hamburg

Business was done in the open air. Whether it was sun, rain, or snow, my mother had to work. I spent so much time at these markets, and I was fascinated by the different ways that the sellers hawked their goods.

By the mid- to late sixties, my mother had saved enough money to start selling cutting torches for a French company. At that point, she had another ingenious idea: she would focus on selling to shipyards. This was a bold move, as women were not supposed to be allowed in shipyards, due to the belief that they brought bad luck.

However, my mother was determined. She polished enough doorknobs to get her foot in the door, and she soon realized that the cutting torches were not the right product for shipyards. What they needed was new shipyards.

It was one of her trips in the early seventies that changed everything for her, transforming her life—and, later, mine as well. After she communicated the need for new shipyards to the Russians, they commissioned her to buy new shipyards in the West. When she returned from one of her trips in January 1974, she had a multi-billion-dollar order in her hands. This was the breakthrough for my mother, an engineer with the experience of a simple market woman. Overnight, she became one of the most influential people in the German steel industry and shortly after, her picture was in many major newspapers.

My mother's story is an inspiration to me. From her humble beginnings in Hamburg, she built a thriving global business, one which was to affect the course of my life drastically, many years down the line. But whatever lay ahead, I believe it was at those early markets that I first learned how to sell, how to persevere—sun, rain, or snow.

I learned so much from my mother, and I never had to suffer her turning around and making me feel like the challenges in her life—all the work to stay afloat, all the struggles—were my fault. She took ownership of her life, and the way she set me up for a successful life of my own was by setting me that incredible example. Hard work pays off—you don't have to hate it, and you don't have to take it out on those around you when things are hard. You can be open and honest, and you can believe life is about more than just getting by—just scraping. You can reach out and grasp everything you dream of. You can make it happen for yourself, no matter if there are people out there who think you can't, or even that you shouldn't. My mom wasn't driven by greed, but by compassion. And, single-handedly, she presented me the world.

Corbinian's letter to Omi Gila

Wisdom is passed down from generation to generation, but it's a beautiful thing when you realize your children have not only learned lessons that have been filtered through their parents' lens, but also inherited wisdom and spirit from their grandparents directly.

This was brought home to me when my son Corbinian brought home a school project in March 2018. It was a letter written to "Omi Gila," my mother.

In the letter, which you can read in the appendix of this book, Corbinian described a day in his life—his daily routine. He would walk our two Parson Russell terriers every morning, and until reading his letter I didn't know that when he did so, he would always call my mom. His letter spoke about their conversations, and I was moved to recognize the lessons he had absorbed.

My mother taught me determination. "Be laser-focused," she always told me. "Be clear about what you want. Have a noble aspect, and don't wish for bad things. If you wish for bad things, then bad things will happen. Be clear about what you want to achieve, what you would like to have. To have it, you have to bring it into your life like it is already there."

What my mom was talking about here was the power of manifesting. She always wanted a child, she told me, so she envisioned that reality for herself. Long before I arrived, she spoke to me as though I was already there. She behaved as though her child was already in her life—and the longed-for baby followed.

It was a nun, Sister Herforth, who taught my mother quintessence—what it means to possess the essence of something. If you believe you have it, if you believe in your goals and are clear about your goals, then they are within your grasp. You will achieve everything you want.

It was through Sister Herforth that my mom found her way to God. *"Ask and it will be given to you; seek and you will find; knock and the door will be opened to you,"* says Matthew 7:7; *"Therefore I tell you, whatever you ask for in prayer, believe that you have received it, and it will be yours,"* says Mark 11:24. You don't have to be religious to understand the meaning behind those messages—put simply, it's the law of attraction.

So, for me, it translated into prayer. Growing up with a single mother, I got to spend so much time with her one on one, and witness her creating a happy family, a successful business, a meaningful life. From that, I too learned the power of manifesting. Focus on what you want, believe that you have it, and it will follow. You can bring your desires to life.

This lesson had always guided me, and reading my son's letter reminded me where some of my core beliefs originated from. I was greatly moved to see how my son had inherited this wisdom, receiving the guidance from my mom's own lips.

Growing pains

In life, it isn't always about the shoes you wear, but the steps you take—and believe me, not all of mine were graceful. Growing up wasn't a bed of roses, and my youth had its fair share of thorns. My mom, bless her heart, made monumental sacrifices, but even though our home was filled with love, it wasn't without its disagreements.

When I was just nine, my mother's travel-heavy job made a suitcase my constant companion, and boarding school my new home—and, to put it mildly, the transition wasn't smooth. I was one of the youngest kids there, and my already, shall we say *spirited* nature was not at all tamped down by my new sur-roundings. My kindergarten teacher, Mrs. Landgraf, once commented to my mom, "I have twenty chil-dren: ten kids and . . . Tino." Yes, I've always had a knack for standing out.

Things weren't helped when I reached drinking age—which, incidentally, is a subject that comes up commonly at the dinner table with my sons Corbin-ian and Caspar, given that we live in America but I was raised in Germany, where a sixteen-year-old can legally enjoy a beer. And believe me, that was a pro-vision I took full advantage of, and not just with beer. Cue the chaos of my teenage years.

Picture this: a bunch of sixteen-year-olds in 1986 in Schloss Stein, Bavaria, my second boarding school, with the rebellious idea of introducing tequila to a very traditional setting—the grand castle that housed the school. One brave (or perhaps foolish) soul snuck in a bottle, complete with lemons and salt, setting the stage for a night that seemed straight out of a teen movie—but movies often gloss over the aftermath. Let's just say that tequila might have been the star that night, but we weren't prepared for its potent performance. One thing led to another, and, in our merriment, a friend accidentally tumbled into the castle's well.

The tale of our tequila-fueled night might evoke a chuckle now, but the repercussions were far from funny. The letter that landed on my mother's desk was my temporary exit pass from the school. My mother's reaction? A tempest of worry, anger, and disappointment. To her, it was more than teenage antics—it was me jeopardizing the education she had fought so hard to give me.

Later in the year, when I arrived at my dad's place to spend the summer, his reaction was somewhat different. "We never got a chance to talk about it," he said. "What happened there?"

I sighed, expecting another telling-off; the one I'd gotten from my mom still echoed. "Well, someone brought in a bottle of tequila."

He chuckled. "Ah, now I understand."

"What do you mean?" I asked.

"Tequila! Tequila is difficult."

"Yeah, no kidding," I muttered.

"We're Baltic!" he exclaimed. "We drink vodka."

That night, he expanded my education in a different way—with lots and lots of vodka.

Because of what happened to his own parents—a story I'm about to tell you—my father pretty much grew up in Great Britain. To me, as a child, it seemed he spoke English better than he did German, and he came across as a perfect British gentleman. Though he was present in my life, and I learned a lot from him, we didn't have many father-son bonding moments, so learning to shoot and hold my vodka—and being taught the importance of context when it comes to enjoying certain pursuits—is a memory I'll always treasure.

In the story of our lives, sometimes it's the missteps that teach us the most. And while this chapter of my tale had its rough patches, it is a poignant reminder of the journey and the people who've shaped me.

Tino and grandmother "Ozi"

Learning of a legacy

In the labyrinth of memories, some stories stand tall, their shadows touching the far corners of our hearts. These tales are more than just anecdotes from the past, they're intrinsic to our identity. The story that follows is one such deeply personal narrative, a tale of valor, sacrifice, and profound love.

My grandmother, Baroness Elisabeth von Freytag-Loringhoven, was born in 1909. My father was her youngest son, the last of four brothers. Perhaps this is why she took a special interest in my upbringing once I came along.

We became close after I went to attend my second boarding school, which was near Salzburg, where she lived. Far away from the rest of my family, I would visit my grandmother—who I called "Ozi"—when I wasn't in school, and she told me many stories. And when I was old enough, she told me about my grandfather, *Wessel* Baron *Freytag von Loringhoven*—about a legacy that couldn't help but influence my life.

One sunny day in the spring of 1985, Ozi took me to her old home—a genuine mansion, not the tiny apartment in the city she was in now. The property had been taken over by the forestry department, and I couldn't imagine what it would have been like to live on such a vast tract of land, surrounded by trees. As we stood together in the back yard, she spoke about my grandfather.

In 1944, my grandfather played an instrumental role in the July 20 plot to assassinate Hitler, which was known as Operation Valkyrie. Although he had worked his way up to the rank of colonel in the Reich Army, he had long been disillusioned with Hitler, having witnessed firsthand his barbarous occupation policy in the East, and this ultimately drew him toward the *Widerstand*—the German resistance. In 1943, he was attached to the Office for Foreign Affairs/Counterintelligence in the Armed Forces High Command in Berlin, where he met Claus Schenk Count von Stauffenberg, the eventual leader of the conspiracy, and entered his circle.

It was my grandfather who obtained the captured British explosives that Stauffenberg detonated in the *Wolfsschanze* (Wolf's Lair), Hitler's headquarters near Rastenburg in East Prussia, while the Führer was engaged in a military conference. The plotters thought at first that they had been successful, but happenstance had caused Hitler to escape from the blast essentially uninjured, and the net quickly closed on Stauffenberg and the other members of his circle. Due to this, I never had a chance to know my grandfather except through stories from my grandmother; my father wasn't even one year old when his father died.

Ozi told me my grandfather was once in the basement of their home with others from the resistance who were involved in the plot, when a high-ranking Nazi officer turned up at the door on behalf of Himmler, the leader of the Gestapo and the ss, and the second-most powerful man in the Third Reich. My grandparents' home was one of the few that had train tracks siding the property, which made it especially attractive real estate in wartime, offering a place to camouflage a train.

"I'm here to make you an offer," the officer said. "I want to take over your house."

The man came inside, and it was up to my grandmother to keep him distracted and send him on his way before he noticed anything was amiss. My grandfather was supposed to be on the Eastern front but had returned secretly, sneaking back to attend this meeting. Ozi did not know exactly what was being planned downstairs—she didn't know the details of the plot at that time—but she did know that if her husband and the others were discovered here, it would have serious, even fatal consequences.

"My house is not for sale," Ozi told the officer. "And I don't have any intention to move out." She came up with excuses why Himmler could not move his train onto one of the sidings of their property, pointing out the young children who would be excited by such a development and naturally proud, which would make them likely to share the news. Having the troops coming and going all the time would have been disastrous.

My grandmother spoke with confidence, but she was very scared. She and her eldest son studied the ranks of the ss for days after the visit, worried that what she'd denied them they would come and take by force. But thankfully, the family was spared the loss of their home, for the time being.

So, from my grandmother, and stories of my grandfather, I came to understand true courage from a young age. But I also came to understand that there are different perspectives when it comes to history, and many sides to a story. My grandfather was a noble man. When he conspired to kill the Führer and overthrow his regime in accordance with his principles, he was not only accepting the risk of being discovered, tortured, and killed by the Gestapo, but also of being declared a traitor to his country, embroiled in a conspiracy to overthrow the government in a time of war. But for my grandfather, it was as his friend Stauffenberg said: "The man who has the courage to do something must do it in the knowledge that he will go down in German history as a traitor. If he does not do it, however, he will be a traitor to his own conscience."[2]

For her part, even though my grandmother did not know the details of the plot, she knew that she and her children were endangered by it. Under the Nazis, the spouses and children of all members of the resistance were at risk due to *Sippenhaft* (family liability punishment), which dictated that a whole family shared responsibility for any crime committed by one of its members. Yet even still, she chose to stand beside her husband. She was a member of the resistance in her own right, a strong woman who survived treatment many people couldn't even imagine. Courageous. Noble.

I will never forget how she looked that spring day in the forest in 1985, like she was gazing into the past. Suddenly, someone from the forestry department came out of the building, having spotted us standing in the backyard.

"What are you doing here?" he demanded. "This is private property. You are trespassing."

My grandmother turned around and addressed him calmly. "Young man, I used to live in this house. This was my house, and it was taken away from me."

She stood there as though it was still her house. Strong and brave, she was guarding the door once more, taking a stand.

---

2   Hoffman P. (2008). *Stauffenberg: A Family History, 1905-1944*. McGill-Queen's University Press.

The guy looked at her, and the expression on his face stays with me to this day. He didn't know what to say.

Finally, he said, "Okay. No problem." Then he turned away and left.

That man would have known the history of the place, and what had happened to the family that lived there. After the failed attempt on Hitler's life, my grandmother received a telegram telling her that her husband was dead. She sought more details, but no one would tell her anything. Soon after, she was arrested, separated from my father and his brothers, and imprisoned. The property was seized. Everything was taken away from her.

It later emerged that, in order to escape capture, torture, and execution, my grandfather had committed suicide. While in prison, Ozi learned that her husband had been expelled from the army post-mortem, with a dishonorable discharge. She had no idea what had been done to her children. Only when she was allowed out of her cell to visit the bathroom was she able to communicate with the other women housed in the prison. In an interview published in Dorothee von Meding's book *Courageous Hearts: Women and the Anti-Hitler Plot of 1944*, she recounted an exchange she would never forget, in which Mika Stauffenberg asked, "Do you also think that they will use the children for medical purposes?"[3] Such were the questions that occupied Ozi in her cell.

---

3   Meding, Dorothee von. (2008) *Courageous Hearts: Women and the Anti-Hitler Plot of 1944*. E-book. Berghahn Books. https://hdl.handle.net/2027/heb08689.0001.001

Some of the women my grandmother was imprisoned with learned—while in captivity—of their children's fates, their husbands' deaths. And, naturally, they feared for their own lives. When that thought took root with my grandmother, however, she decided, "My chief wish was to die a creditable death, and I tried to visualize what it would be like to put one's head in a noose and what dying creditably meant. I resolved to hold my head up high and pray fervently."[4]

When she was released, she made her way to Salzburg, to her mother. My great-grandmother showed her a letter she'd received from Himmler saying her son-in-law had condemned himself; the inquiry was complete, and now they would have to wait and see whether Ozi was involved in the plot. Her children, however, would be returned to my great-grandmother. It turned out that they had been placed in an enforced stay at the Children's Home at Bad Sascha, given a false surname, and told horror stories to stop them from running away. My father was only a baby.

While my grandfather didn't survive the aftermath of that fateful day, his legacy did. And my grandmother, a reservoir of strength, held her family's world together, navigating life's treacherous waters with four sons in tow. The tales she shared about my grandfather weren't merely recollections, but lessons—about bravery, about sacrifice, about the choices we have to make. As a child, absorbing these

---

4   *Ibid.*

narratives sometimes felt overwhelming, a complex web of emotions I wasn't always equipped to untangle. Yet time has a way of bringing clarity, and as the years rolled by, Ozi's words, her feelings, and the enormity of it all began to crystallize in my mind.

So, why reveal such a deeply personal history? Because it's integral to understanding the tapestry of values, beliefs, and ethos I've inherited. The tales of my ancestors are not just remnants of the past, but also guideposts for the future. Their experiences remind me, and now you, of the significance of our family histories and the broader arc of time itself. History, both global and personal, becomes a wellspring of lessons that hold relevance in every era.

Today, as a father, I often find myself pondering the weight of such choices. I gaze into the eyes of my eldest son, named in honor of his great-grandfather, and wonder—faced with such monumental decisions, what path would I tread? It's a thought that hangs heavy, for the choices we make sculpt the challenges that lie ahead. And while it's easy to appraise situations from a distance, when we are in the heat of the moment, decisions become daunting.

In sharing this story, I hope to underscore one pivotal truth: our choices, no matter how confounding, always leave an indelible imprint. It's imperative that we approach them consciously, aware of the ripples they send forth. For in understanding the past, we become better equipped to shape the future.

Choosing from the menu

My grandmother closed her interview with Doro-thee von Meding by saying, "I believe nobody will think badly of me if I say that, for me, 20 July means first and foremost the end of my life with my hus-band. Afterwards, my most important job was to give my sons all the help in my power to make some-thing of their lives."[5] I believe this says a lot about her character.

When I was young, my mom and I had the oppor-tunity to go on holiday with Ozi a couple of times. Though my parents didn't spend much time together, my mom and my dad's mom became close once they met, after my grandmother turned up on our door-step unannounced to see me for the first time.

I remember we were once in the Mediterranean. I was seven or eight, and I couldn't make up my mind what I wanted for dinner. You know how kids can be—I couldn't decide. When Ozi asked, "So what will it be?" I shrugged and answered, "I don't know."

She looked at me. "Okay. If you don't tell me what you want, then you will have nothing."

I didn't tell her what I wanted. "Okay, nothing," she said.

My mom and my grandmother's dinners arrived. Of course, when that happened, I wanted something too. "I want spaghetti," I said.

---

5   *Ibid.*

My mom wasn't exactly easygoing, but she wasn't super-strict. She was about to order me spaghetti, but Ozi intervened.

"No. You had your chance. I asked you several times, and you didn't answer. You didn't know... so now, no."

It was one of those stories my mom loved to tell my children—and one they still remember. I learned my lesson, and ordered when I was asked next time. The point is, the lesson wouldn't have stuck if my grandmother had given in. That wasn't her way. She was disciplined.

From Ozi, I learned the value of following through.

Dinnertime conversation

Let me tell you about another dinner before we leave this chapter of my life. Some years ago, dear friends in Toronto invited my wife and me to their kid's bar mitzvah, though in the end, unfortunately, only I could go. The night before, they hosted an enormous dinner, fifty or sixty people, the whole extended family. I was sat next to one of my friend's aunts.

She asked me about myself, and, as you do, I told her where I was from—Germany. The table went quiet, and heads turned toward me. There was surprise that I was there, since I wasn't Jewish, and even more surprise since I was German. Some comments started coming out about the "bad Germans."

At the time of writing, we've seen Harrison Ford reprise his role as legendary archaeologist Indiana

Jones in *Indiana Jones and the Dial of Destiny*, which obviously wanted to hit the traditional beats that made the original films such a success. So, who are our baddies this time around? The Nazis, again—which, to many, still means simply, "the Germans."

When I was fourteen, my father sent me to England for a summer to learn the language. Living with an English family who spoke no German, I learned quickly, but the language wasn't all I learned. The children over there treated me horribly. They referred to me as "the Nazi" and greeted me with "Heil Hitler!" We were all just kids, but it had a big effect on me at the time. Many things reinforced for me that the Germans are always the bad guys. All Nazis were bad people, right? So, since all Nazis were German, that leads to the fallacy that all Germans were Nazis—and, then, to the "logical" conclusion that all Germans are bad people.

The author and philosopher Bernhard Schlink has spoken about this collective guilt the nation carries, the burden of being shackled to this horrific past, responsibility for such evil. Generation to generation, it is experienced to different degrees, and is wrestled with on both a national and an individual level. In a 2012 article in *The Guardian*, Schlink wrote, "Already, I see that my son has a different relation to the German past than I did. But even my two granddaughters [aged four and eight] will still have to cope with it. When they go abroad and go to Britain and see all these movies that still deal with 'bad Germans'... they will have to find a way to cope with it, and to understand that at least what they owe others is a sense of tact. They will have to learn where this anger comes from, that it comes from real wounds that still torment people."[6]

That anger is valid, and, as Schlink observes, it is hard as a German to reconcile the guilt we have inherited with one's place in the world. But what my grandfather's story taught me is that life is more complicated than black and white. As the war with Ukraine rages on while I write this book, Russia are the bad guys. So, do we now believe all Russians are bad?

I think it doesn't pay to generalize, even though that's what we all have a tendency to do. What choice are we given, when these assorted generalizations, beliefs, and ideologies are imposed on us from a young age? Depending on where and when we grow up, they differ, but the end result is the same. We end up conditioned. We are formed by these biases, shaped by them, and it takes us a lot to get to a point where we question what we believe, and why.

At my friend's celebration, at the dinner table, I spoke a little about my family story. A gentleman stood, raised his glass, and toasted my grandfather. "*Mazel tov! Salut!*"

The other people around the table stood as well, but that had not been my intention in telling the

---

6   Connolly, K. "Bernhard Schlink: Being German is a huge burden," *The Guardian*, 2012. Accessed online 1 August 2023. https://www.theguardian. com/world/2012/sep/16/bernhard-schlink-germany-burden-euro-crisis

story. I just wanted to remind everyone that we should make up our own minds about other people by finding out about their values, their beliefs, what they stand for, and not make assumptions about what they represent. Whole groups of people should not be tarred with the same brush. We can't assume that because we know where someone has come from, we know all about them. It's up to us to learn the truth about each other.

Looking back at my upbringing and the family members who have most influenced the direction of my life, it is clear to me where many of my inherited beliefs and values have come from. The beacon of self-awareness shines a light on the tapestry of my life, and I see the elements that began to shape me. When you examine the stories of your childhood and upbringing, can you identify those first stitches, and who held the needle and thread? What were you told and taught as you grew up—and even once you became an adult?

2

A HARMONY
TO LIFE

I N THE grand theater of life, some of us are born
with a script handed down through generations.
My opening act? An entrepreneurial spirit, inherited from my indomitable mother. Heading from
childhood escapades into my first youthful business
ventures, success and I had a flirtatious relationship to start with, but things soon got serious—and
as any seasoned lover can tell you, intense passion
can sometimes eclipse the finer nuances of a relationship. A stern headmaster, the vibrant allure of
Mexico—these were not mere episodes in my life,
but profound teachers. They whispered lessons of
consciousness and the delicate art of seeing life as
something beyond balance—as a harmonious whole.

There were moments, amidst the intoxication of success, where I danced too fast, losing sight of the real rhythm of life. My fervor sometimes led me down a path where I became a stranger to myself. And isn't that the ultimate paradox—being so engrossed in the dance that you forget the music? As we proceed deeper into this chapter, I invite you to waltz with me through tales of ambition and awakening, as we uncover the beacon of harmony. In the end, living a life of clarity, consciousness, and compassion is not just about the steps you take while swept up in the dance, but also about the moments you pause to truly listen.

From what I can remember, I first ventured into business on a summer's day in 1976, when, at age seven, I organized a garage sale for the kids in my neighborhood. Taking a leaf out of Mark Twain's book, I channeled my inner Huckleberry Finn. Where Huck cleverly convinced the other kids to pay him for the privilege of painting a fence he was punished to paint, I set up a little marketplace for kids to sell their toys—with the catch that they had to give me a little something in return.

It wasn't mischief that led me down this path, merely the entrepreneurial spirit bubbling within. However, it soon became evident why there's an age requirement to conduct business—let's just say, I wasn't quite there yet. Our market was quickly shut down by our parents, who were far from thrilled with my pre-digital version of eBay. But from then on, I was always filled with ideas. Not for nothing had I watched my mom haggle in the markets when I was little: I learned early that business was based on deals, and deals were based on communication, on making connections—on relationships.

As a businessman and investor before I trained as a coach, I had times when I met with resounding successes and times when I crashed and burned. But I wouldn't take back any of those "failures," despite the pain they caused at the time. Even more than each and every triumph, each and every bump, pothole, roadblock, and diversion along the route (*"Do not pass Go, do not collect $200"*) was a lesson.

Golf lessons

At school, I experimented, getting experience doing a few different things. I started a school magazine, I started the theater group, and I became pretty active socially. Throughout my time there, I also played golf. But there was a turning point when I decided to take that latter activity a step further.

In 1985, I had a thought: "How cool would it be if there was a competition we could be a part of?" We had all these school sports, school soccer matches, and school this and school that, but there was no such thing when it came to golf. So, I thought, "Why not initiate an amateur golf championship with the other boarding schools?"

I presented the idea to our headmaster, Olaf Ziegler. Mr. Ziegler ("Olaf" to us kids only when he wasn't within hearing range) listened, and gave me the green light.

"Well, let's try it," he said. "Try and see how far you get."

That was all the permission I needed. I turned over every fricking stone possible. I got in touch with the only golfing magazine in the country, calling them from the yellow phone booth outside the school, using a pile of coins. (No emails, no internet back then.) Having called them, I then had to send them a letter outlining my idea, but I ultimately convinced the chief editor to support me. In fact, he loved it: he said it was a great idea, and confirmed that there had never been an amateur golf championship in Germany at all, for either kids or adults. We would be the first one.

He asked if I'd spoken to the German Golf Association, and when I said I hadn't, he replied, "Don't—don't speak to them."

"Why?" I asked.

"Because they will do everything they can to take it away from you," he answered. "Here's what we do. We'll do this together. I'll support you. I'll give you PR."

Things got rolling from that point. I had spoken to several potential sponsors by then, and while nobody was interested yet, I didn't give up. I did everything from that yellow phone booth, and the tide finally turned when I called up Audi. I had somehow gotten hold of their marketing guy, and I kept calling till I wore him down.

"Look," he said. "You need to convince me."

It was the moment I'd been waiting for. "Here it is," I said. "First, I've got the one and only golf magazine in the country to be the presenter, which gives you PR. That's number one. Number two, I'm going to bring you the customers who will one day decide whether or not to buy your car. They'll remember you supported us. Number three, you get to present your philosophy—*Vorsprung durch Technik* ('Progress through technology')—in a whole new arena."

I concluded, "This is an advantage over the competition I'm offering you. Never before has there been an amateur championship. You would be the company that sponsors the first-ever amateur golf championship in Germany."

Perhaps I didn't really convince him—perhaps he just said yes so I would finally leave him alone. But I didn't care, because at the end of the day, I got him. I got the sponsors I needed, went back to Mr. Ziegler, and presented everything to him. The golf magazine editor came down to visit our school. The country club supported it. And so, we began to plan the tournament.

At that point, the German Golf Association contacted us. They gave me a whole long speech about how it wasn't possible. They told me I couldn't do it, that I wasn't regulated. They gave me a whole bag of bullshit.

"These guys are old-school farts," the editor said, giggling.

"I don't care what they say," I replied. "I'm going to do it. There's literally no law prohibiting it. I'm thinking about rolling it out through all schools. I want to roll it out through all of Germany."

We pushed it through and held the country's first amateur golf championship in 1986—a competition that's still alive and thriving today.

Naturally, the year after the first edition, I was fired up to arrange the whole thing again. But when I spoke to Mr. Ziegler, he said no.

"I'm not allowing that," he said.

I couldn't believe my ears. I was devastated. I didn't get it. The tournament had been successful—everything had been great. But I needed his blessing. I probably had some choice words to say about Olaf, but out of earshot.

I was set to graduate in a year, so I decided I would go back to it once I left school. But the question remained: Why had he stopped me?

When I graduated in 1989, Mr. Ziegler took me aside.

"I know that there's something between us that is not resolved," he said. "Why I didn't allow you to launch your golf tournament again."

"Yeah," I replied, wondering where this was going.

"Do you know why I did that?" he asked.

I shook my head. "No, of course not."

"Well, here's the problem," he said. "All through school, you'd been completely successful in everything you started. When you started the newspaper, I thought it wouldn't last one edition. But two years later, you were still publishing, putting out a paper every two months. You even got the local businesses to support you, paying for advertisements. I said, this is never going to work out, but for whatever reason, you set up shop in that little phone booth."

"Mm-hmm," I said, not getting it.

"I don't even know how you managed to send faxes through the school fax machine. I don't know how you pulled it all off, but you did. And then you started the theater group." He paused. "The first year, I thought, well, let's see how he does. And it was a success. Then you ran for president of the student body, and won. And so it went on."

He took a breath. "When you started your golf tournament, I never thought in my wildest dreams that it would be as huge as it became. It was a triumph. And yet, I decided to stop you." He studied me gravely. "Sometimes, life is just not fair. And I decided you needed to learn that lesson. Success can go to your head, make you think life is always this one-way road, no roadblocks. But that is not the case. You didn't appreciate it at the time, and you may not understand now, but one day you will. Learning how to manage when someone tells you 'no' can be more valuable in life than always hearing 'yes.' And that's what I wanted to teach you. No one is unstoppable. And it's how you face adversity that is the making of you."

With all the fervor of youth, I believed I was invincible. Much like Icarus, I soared high, brushing away cautionary tales and warnings, thinking the sun's scorching rays wouldn't singe my wings. Despite my lackluster skills in Latin, I knew the tale all too well. But, like many young souls, I failed to apply its wisdom to my own escapades. I was audacious, bursting with ambition, with few real setbacks to humble me.

With his age-won wisdom, Mr. Ziegler was trying to anchor me. His words, which, in my youthful brashness, I easily dismissed, were infused with genuine concern. Today, with the advantage of hindsight, I can't help but be profoundly thankful for his attempts to ground my adolescent exuberance. He saw the impending pitfalls that my naivete blinded me to.

Mr. Ziegler is no longer with us, but if, by some cosmic possibility, he's listening, I want to send my gratitude echoing through the universe. He was right. At the time, his advice was a puzzle I couldn't piece together. Life's trials were yet to batter my shores. But as the years have rolled on and as the challenges have mounted, there's many a time I've reflected on that pivotal moment. The essence of his warning, lost on my younger self, resonates with clarity today.

THE SECRET OF
TRUE HARMONY

An early wake-up call in Mexico

You know what one of the biggest myths of the working world is? The myth of work-life balance. There is no such thing. It's such a funny concept. Like thinking when you were a kid that your teachers just existed when they were teaching your class, as if they popped up out of a box while you were there and then got put away again. No—each and every one of your teachers had their own lives, their own challenges and dreams, struggles and triumphs. That day they told you off in class and it didn't feel fair? Maybe it wasn't about something you did, but something that had been done to them, something they were going through elsewhere. And it's the same with work.

When we grow up, we go to work. The old paradigm says, "Leave your home life at the door." At work you're at work. No emotions, no feelings here, just business. All business. It's your professional life. Like you change lives like you change coats when you come through the door. There's a saying in Germany that translates to, "Work is work and schnapps is schnapps." It's about this separation of life and work (as though you don't spend a vast amount of your life at work!).

This is an outdated concept. It needs overhauling. It is possible to have a harmonious life in which all the different parts of you are brought under the same umbrella. People say, "the company this, the company that," but a company is just a legal framework.

What really makes a company? It's a collection of people. People cooperating. People making decisions. You say, "the company hired me," or "the company fired me." No—a person did, or a group of people by committee. A company is a collection of people in relationships with one another.

The thing is, at the end of the day, you're the same you, whatever hat you think you're wearing, or persona you're putting on. What has affected you at home will affect you at work, and vice versa. It all comes back to relationships. If you work with people who make you feel bullied—if you are abused and taken advantage of—it spreads like a virus through your whole world. It's not possible to live a happy, harmonious life at home, simply leaving such issues at work, and vice versa. Say you are deep in a big argument with your partner and you leave to go to work. Do you really switch it off? Or does it affect your day?

How to communicate, how to form relationships, how to connect with people—it all comes back to the same principles, and they apply to all walks of life. If you work like a dog and think it's just your choice to neglect your "home life," don't be proud of it. Half the people you think you're impressing don't even notice; the other half don't really care.

Here I was, young and eager, studying business at college, with the opportunity for a year's sabbatical before heading to Syracuse. I spent six months at BSN (now Danone), traveling between Munich and what was then Czechoslovakia, before taking the chance to work at Colgate in Mexico in the spring of 1992.

I had some Spanish, and I was attracted to spending time in Latin America. But what did I do when I got there? I figured I was there to work, so I worked—long, long hours, hard, hard grinds.

One day, well past 6:00 p.m., Mario Puente, the head of department, came up to me. "What are you doing here?" he asked.

I looked at him, nonplussed. "Working."

"No, no, no, no," he replied. "You have to enjoy life!"

"What do you mean?" I asked.

He smiled at me. "You don't have a girlfriend?"

"No, no," I said, followed by—wait for it—"Colgate is my girlfriend."

The smile was struck from his face by the stunned look he gave me. "Okay. I have to do something here."

Two days later, he took me and some others from the department out for a proper Mexican dinner. It was the best night ever, but needless to say I didn't feel so great the next day.

"How did you enjoy it?" Mario asked when I showed up for work in the morning.

"Oh, it was great!" I exclaimed. "But I had a bit to drink…"

He grinned. "You don't look too healthy. Here's what you do. You go home now. Take the day. But I want you to spend it thinking about life. Then come back."

I did what he said. Driving back to my place up the mountain, I realized what he meant. I was here in this amazing country, and all I did was head to work at 6:00 a.m., driving down the mountain into the smog. And then in the evening, after work, I would drive back out of the smog and up the mountain. I needed to branch out.

Not long after, a colleague introduced me to a girl called Sofia. "We should have lunch," she said.

I never usually left the factory for lunch, so I decided to go for it. When she got in touch to see if I was free, I agreed to meet her.

There was a presentation that afternoon, so I went to tell Mario where I was going.

"That's great!" he said. "See you tomorrow."

"Huh?" I said. "What do you mean, tomorrow? There's the presentation this afternoon."

He looked at me funny. "You'll be back by then?"

"Of course!" I said.

"But you said you're going out for lunch..."

"Yes, just lunch! Not lunch and dinner! I'll be back."

He smiled. "Okay."

I left, kind of confused, and met Sofia at the restaurant.

We started chatting, but it wasn't long till I was chafing to order. This wasn't a business meeting, obviously, but we still had to keep it efficient. As soon as I could do so while still being polite, I broke into the flow of conversation and suggested we choose off the menu.

It took a while to get a server, but we ordered. I relaxed, but not for long. What I learned that day was that lunch in Mexico is always a long lunch.

Nobody rushes. It was a cultural difference I hadn't experienced before.

"Wow," I said, looking at the time. "The food is taking forever here." I was getting nervous.

"Relax!" she said. "We're having lunch! Is there anything else you'd like to order? Do you want a drink?"

"A drink?!" I said. "I can't drink. I have to get back to work."

She frowned. And the more worked up I got, the more I rushed things, the more insulted she became. We'd barely finished eating when I ordered the bill, and we rushed back to the office. She took a wrong turn on the way. I could barely contain myself.

I could tell she was mad, but I couldn't tell why. I'd been nothing but nice the whole time. I'd paid. And I'd clearly missed the presentation I'd told her about.

I charged back into the office and headed straight for Mario. "I'm so sorry! The restaurant took forever. And then Sofia took the wrong way back…"

Mario looked at me and laughed. "Tino, you have to learn so much about our country. You don't go for lunch with a beautiful woman and rush back for presentations. It's not important! Life, I told you."

Even today, I can see the huge smile that Mario had on his face.

"When you think about it, really," he said, "there are two different mentalities. One is the 'curious about life' mentality. And the other one is the 'you've got to do, do, do' mentality."

It was after that moment that I truly began to change a few things. I started to realize that I was missing so much. I wasn't being present in the moment. I began to understand that I was in Mexico to enjoy the country, to learn about the people, to drink a tequila, eat the food, enjoy the atmosphere, go and take a walk on the weekends, see new places. I started to make friends, and we went exploring everywhere. I had the best time ever. And I met the nicest people. Warm, welcoming people who invited me into their homes. I did get a girlfriend (though I wasn't able to retrieve my standing with Sofia—I'd blown that one), and I really learned the language. I thrived—in everything I was doing. The thing is, it wasn't about achieving some mythical work-life balance—it was about embracing the harmony, the wholeness, of life and taking that into every aspect of every day.

Life, in all its intricate beauty, is a gift we often take for granted. It isn't a binary choice between work and leisure; it's a harmonious blend. Yet, in our fast-paced world, we're so often absent from the now. Our minds wander, lost in distant thoughts or propelled by fleeting desires, much like those who view a glorious sunset solely through their camera lens, attempting to seize the moment digitally. They miss out on the raw, visceral experience of just being there. In this digital age, we're ensnared in the illusion that capturing moments on our devices equates to living them. The truth? True living lies in immersing oneself fully, feeling every sensation, and cherishing every second.

Mario and Mexico taught me to be present, wholly and completely, and let life's harmony envelop me.

Not enough hours in the day

As is so often the case, sometimes you need to learn a lesson more than once. And for me, being a workaholic has been a hard habit to break.

One of the first runaway successes I experienced put some lessons in stark relief—not just about the dangers of running yourself into the ground through working, but also about how you can respond if your values are being tested.

My boss at BSN was a guy called Rolf Glöckler, who was to become one of my great friends and business partners. Rolf was a whirlwind of creativity and determination, the kind of man who colored outside the lines and made it look effortlessly cool. As a university student, while his peers slogged through assignments, Rolf was hustling, running a lively bar and operating cable cars. His ambitious spirit found its zenith when he became a marketing prodigy at Henkel KGaA in Düsseldorf. Ever the trailblazer, Rolf was at the heart of an advertising revolution, always pushing boundaries.

Following my work experience in Mexico, I went back to college to complete my degree. After graduation, I was accepted onto the international Colgate Global Trainee Program, and my family were pleased.

I was pleased too! But then I got a call from Rolf in the spring of 1994. He'd just joined Löwenbräu AG, one of the world's most famous breweries, based in Munich.

"There's lots of things going on here," he said. "I want you to come on board. I need someone I can trust. Come back and work for me."

As a young man with an unyielding spirit, I gazed upon the color-coded trifecta of folders Colgate-Palmolive had handed me. They weren't just folders—they were a meticulously charted trajectory of the next five years of my life. If I followed it, I could predict my exact location in the corporate landscape. But the rebel in me balked at the idea of tracing these predetermined paths. I didn't see myself sketching out road maps—I yearned for the uncharted, the unscripted. The thrill of my adventures in Mexico still pulsed through my veins, igniting a craving for more, an insatiable hunger to explore vast horizons. And who better to guide me than the maverick who'd revolutionized advertising in Germany? The Colgate program, while globally esteemed, oozed structured corporatism. On the other hand, there was Rolf's tantalizing unpredictability. The decision felt like a fork in the road, but deep down, my adventurer's heart knew its true north. I trusted my instincts, and dove headfirst into the unknown.

Not long after heading back to Germany to start working with Rolf, I received a call from an old school friend.

"Have you heard of Red Bull?" he asked me.

Crazy to think of it now, but I hadn't. Very few people had at the time.

"Never heard of it," I said. "What's the deal?"

"It's an energy drink," he explained, "and the reason I want to talk to you is a dear friend of my father's has developed one of his own. Same, same, but different. He's called it Flying Horse."

"Never heard of it either!"

"You have to go there," my friend said. "He owns a small brewery up in North Bavaria. He's big in mineral water supply for highway point of sale."

In Germany at the time, all the shops closed at 6:00 p.m. If you wanted a drink after that, you had to go to a convenience store or a gas station. These were the outlets where the business stocked its mineral water and multivitamin water. This was a sizable undertaking.

I was interested. The point of difference with Flying Horse was in its taste. Not chemically or anything like that—it was more like drinking apple juice with soda.

I started to look into it, and the more I dug the more interesting it got.

At the beginning, the ingredients in some of the energy drinks being produced were illegal in Germany. The products couldn't be sold in Germany or any European Union country, so they had to be smuggled over borders, and then sold in front of the clubs. They were gaining in popularity, and the restrictions were being challenged.

Working at Löwenbräu, I saw the opportunity. We supplied a lot of restaurants and clubs with beer. What about a new sales channel?

I took it to Rolf. "Here's an opportunity," I said.

He heard me out and got excited. "This is amazing. Let's do this together!"

In the early days, we operated without external investors. Reflecting upon those times, I'm astounded by the unparalleled success we achieved, a feat that's rare in the business world. But while I recognized a success story many only dream of, one of the brand's elderly stakeholders remained skeptical.

He'd never witnessed such a phenomenon, and doubted its potential to last. I, on the other hand, envisioned grand horizons. I dreamt of Flying Horse soaring beyond the heights of Coca-Cola. Fast forward to today, and when you see giants like Red Bull, it's evident my aspirations weren't just flights of fancy. We even became the first energy drink to sponsor a snowboarding event. Back then, though, my ambitions seemed outlandish, to the extent that the stakeholder labeled me mad.

His skepticism grew, and he became intent on milking the brand for all its worth, viewing it merely as a fleeting sensation. A world of possibilities lay at our feet, but I was powerless, lacking the authority to make pivotal decisions. My youthful exuberance, paired with the overwhelming success, sometimes clouded my judgment. In retrospect, I recognize my missteps. I could have proposed buying him out, perhaps. Given his reservations about the brand's longevity, he might have been receptive to the idea. But this is just one example of a different path I could have taken—there were many options. Instead, my stubbornness and inability to foresee a solution led me to drop everything and walk away.

It really takes something to call it out when you see behavior that doesn't align with your values, but it's important to realize that you don't have to accept it. You don't have to make excuses for people, or accept other people's excuses on their behalf. Sometimes it's things you can't change. You can't change someone in that moment—they need to come to some realizations themselves. But you can choose to politely speak up, and you can choose to disengage.

This idea of speaking up is something I really started drumming into my kids after I nearly died of Covid. Unquestioning acceptance, responding with silence, is just not how I operate anymore. If I disagree with something, if I see something out of alignment with my values, I make sure to say so. My kids may have rolled their eyes once or twice at the repetition, but when my eldest son, Corbinian, graduated, he took me to one side.

"Hey, Dad," he said. "I just want to tell you one thing. I really appreciate what you do for me. I understand what you're doing, where you're pushing me and why. Even though I don't always get it right away, I'm grateful for what you're doing. I'm grateful, and I love you."

That, to me, was the best thing I could possibly ever hear. And he didn't just say it to make me happy—he meant it from the bottom of his heart. If I've been able to teach my children such values, to act in alignment with their values and stand up for them, to live nobly, then I have succeeded as a father.

Back then, of course, I didn't have everything figured out. When I walked out on that job, I pretty much walked myself straight into hospital, where I was given another wake-up call.

We called Flying Horse "the twenty-fifth hour," because it gave you another hour in the day. But I'd been spending every one of those twenty-five hours working. I'd made myself unwell.

The doctor walked into my room one day, and I was already back on my phone making business calls.

He just looked at me. "Oh, you guys are the best patients, because I can tell you, you continue to do that, you'll be back here with a heart attack."

He walked out, leaving me to digest that. I had some things to think about.

Today, I realize the weight of my decisions. Ending up in hospital was a result of all the stress I'd brought upon myself. But I could have managed the situation much better, with far less stress—and more success.

I didn't appreciate it at the time, but now I look back and see that life is not a series of pulleys and weights—not a balancing act you need to perfect to be happy. It's one glorious whole, a symphony of elements that can soar together side by side. The beacon of harmony was present through all of my early experiences in business—I just needed to see the light. When you look at your life, at the relationships and aspirations you've had in the world—not just the world of work, but all of it—what do you see? Have you teetered on a tightrope, trying to maintain a precarious balance at times? Do your stories reveal the connections between seemingly disparate aspects of life?

3

BUILDING BLOCKS
OF SELF-BELIEF

<hr>

ELF-BELIEF IS A powerful beacon that can illuminate a structure that supports you through life's quakes and trembles. My experiences, from appreciating the synchronicity of diverse cultures in an orchestra to navigating the bustling markets of Vietnam, taught me that unity, ambition, and purpose can come together to form the most incredible architecture. However, my journey wasn't without its shaky moments. The harsh jolt of letting go of a brilliant idea and the deep crack of failure echoing through the dot-com crash met the hushed lullaby we sang my son Corbinian as he came into the world, urging me to rise again.

Through it all, I realized that self-belief is a delicate thing to construct. I'm not talking about the loud trumpeting of arrogance or the careless overtures of hubris. No, true self-belief is a quiet confidence that hums softly, reminding us of our worth, even when faced with the harshest of critiques.

As we delve into this chapter, let's explore the fine line between genuine self-belief and unwarranted egotism. The beacon of self-belief is not just about standing tall, but also about understanding when to bow gracefully, and when to stand your ground.

Marching to your own music

Early in the summer of 1993, when I was home from college, I got involved in a music festival. The Schleswig Holstein Musik Festival is an annual classical music event held in the summer in northern Germany, and my mother helped manage the sponsorship. I had some experience working on a concert as a summer job, and I took on a marketing internship at the festival. It was tiny back then, but now it's one of the largest cultural music festivals in the world.

I'd gathered some ideas while I was studying in the States, and I was eager to put them into practice. My mom had brought on some sizable sponsors, but they had all signed on in the German spirit of *mitsein* (which translates to 'being-with'—a sense of social togetherness); this means they were more like donors, who offered their donations, and then stayed very much in the background.

In America, companies sponsored universities, museums, art. People donated and had hospital wings named after their families. Sponsors were proud to be associated with what they did—their names were shouted loudly everywhere. They talked about what they were doing and why. But in Germany, none of that was really visible. There were quiet donations and patrons, with no names mentioned. Success wasn't shouted about, the donors not wanting to attract envy.

I said, "Hey, these companies who are paying sizable money, we should give them a return on investment."

"What are you talking about?" the organizers asked me. "This isn't soccer. This isn't Formula One."

I fought for the concept, despite more than a few people wondering what this twenty-year-old idiot who'd turned up was trying to do. I showed them my ideas, where banners and logos could go, and demonstrated how it would attract new sponsors to the festival. It was kind of controversial—giving the sponsors some value for their money was a shocking change to the way things had always been done. There was even an article on it in the newspaper. In the end, though, my plans were pushed through, with a lot of elements I initiated staying with the festival for good.

It was great to make a contribution that made a difference like that. But the greatest part about being involved with the festival was the musicians I met. The great maestro Leonard Bernstein founded the festival's orchestral academy, which gave young talent from around the world the opportunity to play with famous musicians and conductors, and be coached and mentored. Over time I got the chance to know Professor Justus Frantz, the conductor of the orchestra and head of the festival. One evening, we attended a dinner where I sat with someone whose parents had spent their life savings to send him over to play for three months under such tutelage.

The dimly lit room of the barn in Wotersen seemed to hum with anticipation as Justus made his way to the small stage. The members of the Orchestra of the Nations sat tuning their instruments, but their eyes were firmly fixed on their renowned conductor. As the first note resonated, I felt the world around me fade. The musicians, from varying backgrounds, faiths, and cultures, played in perfect harmony, their unity transcending the notes.

When the piece concluded, the room erupted in applause. Later that evening, I made my way up to Justus, still in awe of what I'd witnessed.

"Justus," I began, my voice filled with admiration, "that was more than just music. It was a journey, a story, a testament to unity."

He smiled warmly, the passion for his craft evident in his twinkling eyes. "Ah, Tino. Music is the universal language, isn't it? When words fail, melodies speak."

"But how do you do it?" I asked, genuinely curious. "How do you bring together such a diverse group of musicians and create ... magic?"

Justus leaned back thoughtfully.

"Collaboration and communication," he began. "It's like any relationship. You need to listen more than anything."

He placed a reassuring hand on my shoulder. "Life, like music, is filled with highs and lows, crescendos and pauses. Embrace each note, each moment, and always strive to create harmony, both in music and in your relationships. The world needs more maestros who understand the true essence of unity and collaboration."

I nodded, deeply touched by his words. "I'll remember that, Justus. Thank you for sharing not just your music, but the wisdom behind it."

As we parted ways the lingering notes of the orchestra filled the room, but it was Justus's profound insights that echoed in my heart. A lesson on collaboration, communication, and the beautiful symphony of life, learned in the most unexpected of places.

The people I met while I worked at the festival came from a range of different countries, even from war zones, but they were all united in music. It was a wonderful way to bring together so many people from different backgrounds, music functioning as a peaceful common denominator.

I learned a lot about communication, and the power of hearing people's stories. It was a privilege to be able to see behind the scenes and get to know everyone. Bringing youth on board and new ideas from different cultures meant breaking down borders. And while that kind of thing might upset the status quo, the benefits were obvious.

Lost in translation: My audiobook odyssey from America to Germany

My time with the Schleswig Holstein Musik Festival in the early to mid-nineties really proved to me the value of collaboration, and what can be achieved when the same passion is embraced by people eager to make something beautiful together. It's sad to me that people often find themselves in the opposite situation, surrounded by people telling them they cannot do something.

Another idea I brought home from America was the concept of putting books on tape. Audiobooks have come a long way since then, but this was long before podcasts—I'm talking about tapes you'd listen to through a car's cassette player. They were huge over in the States already, on sale everywhere, in every airport.

It was 1993 when I called Tony Robbins.

The greeting at the other end of the line was always the same: "It's a wonderful day at the Tony Robbins Research Center."

I spoke to some of the people there, asking, "Hey, how about going to Germany?"

I approached others, too, and somehow got options to sign on. Looking back, I'm not really sure how I managed it. But one thing people were quick to tell me was that I wouldn't be able to pull it off by myself.

"You don't have the resources," they would say. "You don't have the expertise."

I questioned whether I would be able to execute my vision. So I took the idea to a big company who owned a host of large bookstores.

"Build us a business plan," they said. "We'll take a look and see if it makes sense."

I put together the business plan. I'd been working on this project for a while by then, and I included everything, including the agreements I'd already made. When I presented to the company, they offered me a lump sum and bought the plan from me. It felt like a lot at the time, but I know now it was worth a lot more.

And so the whole thing moved away from me. The company partnered with a publishing house, and when they launched, they launched big.

When I look back on it all, I know that today I could just have done it myself. I let myself be blocked by those who didn't believe in me. I let that affect my own self-belief. They made me think I couldn't follow through.

There were "rules," people told me. "Hey," they said. "You can't do this unless you have a business. You can't do this unless you have a publisher. You can't do this unless..."

This is how my generation grew up, to a large extent—all these negatives. "If you don't already have the ingredients, you can't bake the cake."

Today, the belief that you can't just do things yourself has been dismantled in so many arenas. It's been proven time and again that people can make their dreams a reality. Today, there's little that can stop you from executing an idea that you believe is worth executing.

What would I say to my younger self? Well...

I'd say, "Tino, listen. Anything you see, anything you touch, anything you comprehend—at a certain point in time, it wasn't there. It didn't exist. Anything you can think of, it's possible."

Think of it this way. Everything you're so used to using nowadays—your laptop, your phone, your TV, your car, your house, even—these things didn't use to exist. They started out as a crazy idea. And *then* the ingredients were assembled; *then* the cake was baked.

If everyone trying to achieve something let themselves be blocked, we would never have any progress. The thing is, if you're clear about what *you* want, then you can begin to manifest that. Envision it. Follow your dreams, and your dreams will come.

This is the very same thing that my mother told me over and over again: *Be clear, believe, focus, and it shall be.*

This is where some people get it wrong. You don't just sit and wait around for that to happen—you have to act on your self-belief, and you have to keep up the mental strength to continue no matter what. People will still tell you that you cannot do it, but those people want to keep you small—perhaps because that's what they learned to believe about themselves. But you have to believe in the power to overcome such conditioning.

"It's no good," they'll say about your idea. "You can't do it unless..."

They said the world was flat, but now we know it's round; they said people would never fly, yet now we've been to space. We are brought up restricted, limited, and that can be hard to defy. In the past, some of the greatest minds were committed to mental hospitals. It wasn't till far in the future that people realized they were right all along.

Ignore anyone who tells you your dream is impossible. If you really, really want something, it's yours.

Shipped to Southeast Asia

In the spring of 1996, I was studying for my master's in Phoenix when the phone rang. It was my mom on the line.

"We've got a problem here," she said. "You've got to come back."

"But..." I began. "I'm studying!"

Needless to say, I was never going to win that argument. My mom led with some version of, "It's payback time," and told me I was needed because she'd just opened offices in Southeast Asia.

Over the years, my mother had built her business into a huge success. She'd expanded into many different areas, including shipping and shipyards, energy, medical technology, agricultural machines, automobiles, steel, and power plants. She had offices in Poland, China, India, and now Vietnam. She was the representative for large organizations, such as Deutsche Bank, Volkswagen, Krupp, and MAN.

I pointed out that I didn't know her business; her business was not my business. What use would I be?

It had no effect on her. She simply asked when I'd be back, and said I could pick up my studies again afterward. So that's what I did.

I recall staring out the window of the plane, the vast expanse of the Atlantic Ocean spread out before me. I thought about all the things I had left behind in the United States: my friends, my girlfriend, my unfinished MBA. But I also thought about the possibilities that awaited me. I was excited to start a new chapter in my life, but I was also a little bit scared.

"What if I don't succeed?" I asked myself. "What if I make a mistake?"

I took a deep breath and tried to calm my nerves. "I have to believe in myself. I have to believe that I can achieve my goals."

I closed my eyes and imagined my future. I saw myself graduating from business school, landing a great job, and starting my own company. I knew this would be an important step along the way, and I saw myself making a difference in the world.

When I opened my eyes, I felt a sense of determination. I knew that I could make my dreams come true, but I also knew that I had to work hard. I had done it before—I knew I had to be focused and disciplined. I had to be willing to take risks.

Gradually, I began to get excited for the challenges that lay ahead. I was confident that I could overcome them, and I knew I was ready to start my next chapter in Asia.

I was lucky to meet some great people there—first in Vietnam, and later in Singapore, Thailand, China, and Hong Kong. It was back in the day when you flew into Hong Kong and could still see the laundry outside on the balconies as you were landing. Only a few pilots were allowed to land in Hong Kong's Kai Tai Airport, the island's international airport until 1998.

Just as in Mexico after I'd learned my lesson from Mario, I connected with different cultures and with the people. We got along so well, and it was an honor to be accepted by them. I became a link between the West and Southeast Asia, merging with a shipping company out of Hamburg and becoming their director. This came with a fleet of ten large container ships and a host of new buildings. Integrating our trading organization, we built a new company, which I directed as well.

Returning to the Presidential Palace in Hanoi after three decades. What began as a bold business venture in my twenties evolved into a profound lesson in cross-cultural understanding and the power of genuine connection.

I often had to fly to China and South Korea, where the ships were built, and it was during this time that I had the idea to build a trading house for Vietnam. Everything was government-owned, and it was very difficult for the government to engage in foreign trade with foreign currencies. So I proposed we create a clearing house, which would be owned by the government but could be based outside of the country, and therefore operate differently.

I was invited to present the concept to the president of Vietnam, Lê Đức Anh, the vice president, and the minister of transport at a dinner.

Taking a deep breath, I sat down at the long dinner table. I was seated close to the president, so when the time was right and I was allowed to address him, I could raise the issue. He was sitting at the very end of the table in a big chair.

When the time came, I walked up to him. He sat there in front of me, looking at me with piercing eyes. I felt a wave of nervousness wash over me.

"You can do this, Tino!" I told myself. "So many people are relying on you..." But the thought made me feel even more uncomfortable.

I stood in front of the president, my heart pounding. He didn't say anything, just stared at me. I cleared my throat and began to speak.

"Mr. President," I said, "I'm honored to be here, and I am very grateful to be allowed to talk to you about the idea of establishing a Vietnamese trading house in Germany."

I paused, and the president continued to stare at me. I could feel the eyes of the other people in the room on me too. They were all nervous, just like me.

"I know this is a big idea," I said, "but I believe it could be very beneficial for our country. A trading house in Germany would give us access to new markets and resources. It would also help us to develop our foreign trade capabilities."

I took another deep breath and continued. "I've already done some preliminary research, and I believe this is a viable project. I'm confident that we can make it a success."

I finished speaking and looked up at the president. He was still staring at me, but his expression had softened slightly. I handed him the proposal and our presentation.

"Thank you for your presentation," he said. "I'll need some time to consider this proposal."

I nodded and turned to leave. As I walked back to my seat, I felt a wave of relief wash over me. I had done it. I had faced my fear and spoken up. I looked at our director, my friend Mr. Song. He smiled and nodded like he was saying, "Great job!"

I knew that the president would make the right decision. And if he decided to go ahead with my proposal, I would be ready. I would make sure that the trading house was a success.

After dinner, I walked out of the room and into the fresh air. I took a deep breath and smiled. I had done it. I had had my moment to shine.

Just a few days later, Mr. Song came in holding a fax, with the biggest smile on his face. "You did it, Tino. The president has given us his approval!"

Ecstatic, I began the work. I flew back to Hamburg, went to the town hall, and met with the vice mayor, Dr. Thomas Mirow, the Senator of Trade, and other ministers. They thought I had a screw loose, joked I'd been on the opium. I told them it was going to happen, and they didn't believe me.

I followed through, but the tricky challenge we came up against was assigning ownership. It needed to be an official who could sign for the government. And so the Minister of Trade came to establish the company, and since we also required a representative from Germany, I became one of the directors of the company.

When the consulate in Hamburg was informed that the minister was coming, and the word spread to the town hall in Hamburg and on to the government in Berlin, that's when things got hectic. Everyone thought it was unbelievable, and it made big news.

Overnight they had to arrange a state visit, and we got things up and running. I had established through a contact in Vietnam that there was an initiative instigated by Bill Clinton called the Oil for Food Program, which was being led by the United Nations. As Vietnam was one of the world's largest rice suppliers, to kick things off, I suggested, "Why don't we apply to supply rice?"

My good friend Frank Baehr and I literally trekked across Vietnam, negotiating in the most remote rice fields, convincing wary stakeholders, working tirelessly day and night. His expertise from his family's Agro Trading company in Switzerland and my relentless drive saw us through. We didn't just aim to be part of the initiative—we became the initiative.

Long story short, I was able to get that contract, and Vietnam became the official supplier for the Iraqi Oil for Food Program. Then I had to make sure that we obtained the ships to bring the rice to Iraq.

It was an incredible time, where I learned in depth not only about the shipping business, but also about how to negotiate and communicate effectively across borders. The main lesson, however, was probably more in how to follow an idea through, when there were others who didn't believe in it.

As we've talked about, when something is a new idea—and it looks difficult on top of that—there are always going to be people who encourage you not to try. Sometimes this is kindly meant—they do not want to see you fail. But sometimes it is a failure of imagination of their part: because they could not imagine doing such a thing and achieving such goals, they do not think anyone else capable of it either. Sometimes, when something is big and scary, such people think it isn't worth attempting.

I learned to cultivate the self-belief I needed to overcome such assertions. There are always roadblocks, there are always challenges in anything you try to achieve. The important thing is the attitude with which you face them. You have to earn other people's trust—and to do that, you have to trust in yourself.

When the bubble bursts

When I left Southeast Asia in mid-1999, I knew my time there had been a resounding success. I was on top of the world. Though I'd hit some challenges getting some of my ideas to fly, I probably still wasn't close to understanding what my old headmaster had meant when he set me up to taste true opposition and failure for the first time. (I mean, I did get paid quite handsomely—or so I considered at the time—for that audiobook business plan, after all!) Inevitably, however, the time to learn the value in his lesson was coming.

I exited shipping as I'd always planned, excited about the leaps, bounds, and potential being explored in the tech sector. All of a sudden everyone was an investment banker, a career I'd always wanted to pursue.

"How is this possible?" I said. "I want to do that too!" It almost looked too good to be true.

But like I said, it hasn't all been rainbows. I was hit hard—along with a lot of people—by the dot-com crash of 2000, and then again in the global financial crisis of 2007-08.

When the tech sector was booming, I threw myself into it. I even arranged to meet with a company in San Francisco when I was on my honeymoon in September 1999 (yes, that went down with my wife about as well as you might expect!). I was excited, but I tried to be careful. Those who had jumped on board were suddenly super-successful, acting like they knew more than anyone else. But I feel now that less than one percent of those people really knew what was going on, and very quickly, everything came undone. It was like death by a thousand papercuts. You watched one company fold after another—worth billions one day, gone the next. It felt like the apocalypse: you were sitting in the back of a bus that was heading over a cliff, and there was nothing you could do except try and scramble out, screaming. Reality had never quite lived up to the dream as it was, but no one had guessed this mess could lie at the end of the rainbow. It was devastating.

I hadn't been investing in the tech sector long when the dot-com bubble burst. I'd only just gotten started—it felt like I was the last one to arrive at the party, the guy who walks in holding two bottles of bubbly and waves them around while everyone else is already on their way out. Unfortunately, one of the last people to leave the party also snatched my bottles, so I didn't even have those anymore.

In the fall of 2001, I sat in my small office in Hamburg and pulled my hair out. What had I done?

I'd gotten married a couple of years before. We'd bought our first house, and my first child had only just arrived. I'd lost so much; this was my rock bottom. I didn't know how I was going to put food in the fridge. How was I going to tell my wife?

I'd been through a lot in my life, but nothing had prepared me for this next phase, the biggest failure of my life thus far. I had worked so hard, put in so many long hours, and made so many sacrifices. And for what? Nothing.

I felt like I had let everyone down, especially myself. I didn't know what to do. I felt like giving up.

But then I thought about my wife and my son. I thought about how much they meant to me, and I knew that I couldn't give up. I had to keep going.

THE SECRET OF
TRUE SELF-BELIEF

I took a deep breath and started to talk to myself.

"Tino, you're not a failure," I said. "You're just going through a tough time. Everyone fails sometimes. The important thing is to pick yourself up and keep going."

I remembered past challenges and what they'd taught me.

"You have to believe in yourself," I said. "You have to believe that you can do this. You've been through a lot in your life. You've overcome challenges before, and you'll overcome this one too. You're stronger than you think."

I told myself, "You're a good person. You're a hard worker. You're intelligent. You're capable. You deserve to succeed."

I took a deep breath. "You're going to get through this. I believe in you."

Walking over to the window, I looked out at the trees and the garden in front of me. I knew that it was going to be tough, but I was determined to succeed. I was going to rebuild my self-belief and redefine my purpose. I was going to reinvent myself and pull myself out of this.

I turned away from the window and looked at my son's picture on my desk. I smiled. I knew I had to do this—for him.

I remember too well the storm of emotions I felt. I was feeling angry, sad, even hopeless. But I had to remind myself that these feelings are normal. I had to allow myself to feel my emotions, but not let them consume me.

My next step was to start to rebuild my self-belief. This meant focusing on my strengths and accomplishments. I thought about all the things I had overcome in my life. I reminded myself that I was capable of great things.

I came to realize that we are not alone. Everyone experiences failure at some point in their life. The important thing is to pick yourself up and keep going.

I thought back to my amateur golf tournament. Mr. Ziegler was right: what was important was what I did next. I could either dwell on this defeat, let it eat me up, fall right down that big black hole, or I could look around me, look for new, different opportunities. I could go to work in another way; I could put this behind me and move forward.

I knew that I could do this. I knew that I was stronger than I thought. What I didn't know was that this was just one of many ups and downs I would encounter.

I was contemplating going back into shipping when a friend called with an opportunity to join a project in the energy sector. I struggled with the decision: every choice felt so big after what had happened, especially now that I had a house and a family.

But this was where a mentality I had learned to embrace in Asia came back to help me. The important thing was not to get sucked into the whirlwind of chaos. I needed to stay calm. I needed to distance myself and stay cool.

Think about it: if you called 911 in an emergency, in dire need of help, would it be any use if the person at the end of the line got emotional with you? Instead of the calm, collected response designed to get the right assistance to you as efficiently as possible, what if they freaked out? "God! That's awful! There's someone actually *in your house?* Oh my God, that's terrible!" You'd lose your mind even more.

CONQUERING FEAR

It's not easy to distance yourself from your emotions. Fear is one of the most vicious emotions—it can take you over, it can drown out rational thought. So training yourself to step back from that cliff is key.

Above all, I needed to gain clarity about what I needed, where I wanted to go. I hadn't mastered the art of it yet, but it was a ladder that got me out of a very dark hole.

I got involved in the large energy project my friend had called about, providing advice and connecting the team with key contacts. In return, I earned a consulting fee and a share of the project's success. And it was a *huge* success. Not only was I able to get back on my feet, I was also able to get back into investing. At the same time, I began consulting. I had the experience to help businesses expand internationally, and I coached companies, business owners, and managers through the steps they needed to take to achieve successful global growth.

When the real estate bubble burst, I wasn't as badly affected as I was in the dot-com crash. I had learned the hard way not to put my investment eggs all in one basket, and I got out with a black eye. Okay... maybe two black eyes.

In the summer of 2007, I stared at a message on my phone, my heart sinking. It described how the air conditioning had been shut off in the public areas of a new building in South Beach, Miami, where I had purchased another apartment. Construction had halted everywhere.

I was terrified when I saw the news. I didn't know what was going to happen. I thought about the big economic crisis in 1907, when millions of people lost their jobs. Was this the end? Was this the beginning of a new Great Depression?

I flew to Miami and drove to the building; I wanted to see it for myself. When I arrived, I spoke to a woman who worked there.

She was very concerned. "The elevators are shut down, and people are sleeping in their cars because they can't afford to stay in hotels."

She said that some people had moved into their apartments just in sleeping bags because the buildings weren't ready. There was no money to finish them.

I stood there listening to her, and felt a wave of despair wash over me. This was it. This was the end. The world was falling apart.

I got back in my car and drove back to our apartment in the Portofino Towers in South Beach. I turned on the TV, and all I saw was bad news. The stock market was crashing. Banks were failing. People were losing their jobs. It felt like Doomsday.

I sat there, staring at the TV, feeling numb. I didn't know what to do. I felt like giving up—again. But then I thought about my family. I thought about my children. I looked at a picture of my two boys, Caspar and Corbinian, and I knew that I had to keep going, for them.

I took a deep breath and stood up. I turned off the TV, went to my desk, and started writing. I wrote about what I had seen and heard. I wrote about my fears and my hopes. I wrote about the future. I didn't know if anyone would ever read what I wrote, but I didn't care. I just needed to get it out of my system.

I wrote for hours. When I was finished, I felt a sense of relief. I had faced my fears and put them into words. I knew that I would get through this. The world was changing, but I would change with it. I would find a way to thrive in this new reality.

I knew that I wasn't alone. There were millions of people who were going through the same thing. We would get through this together.

We would rebuild. We would recover. We would come out stronger than ever before. And if there was one country that knew how, it was America. A feeling of hope came over me as I decided what direction to head in next.

Considering my investments, there was one in particular that stuck out for me. It was time to pick something to really sink my teeth into.

Have there been times you've struggled with your self-belief? It's an element that needs building up and nurturing, especially when you've been knocked down. The peaks and valleys of my life have taught me that when you truly believe—in yourself, in your dreams—you can move mountains. The beacon of self-belief shines a light on our every endeavor and shows us our worth.

4

THE COMPASS
OF COMPASSION

M UCH LIKE Miami's unpredictable weather during hurricane season, love and relationships
come in all shades and intensities. Sometimes these connections burn hot and bright
and are over quickly; others are tepid and take their
time fizzling out. Still others endure, whatever the
weather, and navigate life's storms together.

I once dove into the world of online dating, searching for answers in a sea of casual connections.
Yet instead of passionate tales of falling head over
heels in love, I unearthed stories of souls seeking
clarity, yearning for understanding, and wrestling
with desires they could barely voice.

Through this chapter, the beacon of compassion
shines brightly—evident in acts of kindness and tales
of infectious positivity, epitomized by little red shoes,

and lessons from a silver-haired Casanova who taught me that charm is really about listening and genuine connection. Sometimes, the most profound lessons about love come from the most unexpected teachers.

The online dating revolution

Think of a couple heading out on their first date; they're going to the cinema, a classic choice. It's 2007, so in the crowd of moviegoers mingling in the foyer, only about one out of thirty is click-clacking on their techno-chic Blackberry, sending or receiving emails.

Our couple isn't the only pair of young lovebirds—there are many couples in the crowd. Of those in line on first dates, less than ten percent met at church or school. About twenty percent met at a bar or at a restaurant, and another twenty percent met either at work or in college. Somewhere between roughly twenty and thirty percent met through mutual friends.[7]

If you were to ask the other twenty percent where they met, you probably wouldn't get the truth.

"At the Christmas Eve Jewish Singles' dance. We made eye contact and ..."

"It was fate—we met at the *Buffy the Vampire Slayer* binge-a-thon at the YMCA."

"We literally bumped into each other at the noodle stand, in the Ramen Museum in Tokyo!"

---

7   Rosenfeld, Michael J., and Reuben J. Thomas. "Searching for a Mate: The Rise of the Internet as a Social Intermediary." *American Sociological Review* 77, no. 4 (August 2012): 523–47.

Actually, in 2007, twenty-two percent of hetero-sexual couples in line for their respective movies met online. For same-sex couples, it was closer to fifty percent.[8]

So, why the compulsion to lie about where they met? Why not just 'fess up to eHarmony or OkCupid?

Because in 2007, online dating was still new, and it wasn't widely accepted. There was a certain stigma attached to it. It was sort of the relationship equivalent of admitting that you pop your pimples: common enough, but not exactly something to be proud of, and definitely not something that you would discuss in polite company.

But that doesn't mean it was brand new. In 1995, not long after Netscape launched its revolutionary web browser, Match.com offered the first platform for singles to meet online.

The concept caught on quickly in gay communities, especially with males and tech geeks. But before long, the idea had been adopted by a broad assortment of people. As the internet itself became more widely used, online dating grew right along with it.

Soon new sites emerged, many of them targeting niche groups. There was cougar dating, Catholic dating, country music dating, and just about every other kind of dating you can imagine. (Seriously—some of these sites got *specific*.) As this trend was just starting to develop, I realized that online dating was poised to follow the pattern of another massive modern industry: cable TV. Think about it—we used to have three television channels. Now we have thousands,

---

8   Rosenfeld and Thomas, "Searching for a Mate," 523-47.

catering to every interest imaginable, no matter how niche. The world of online dating platforms was on the same path.

What was behind this rapid success? Online dating *worked*. People met potential partners that they actually liked. It was easy and convenient. Hell, compared to being set up with your aunt's neighbor's best friend's weird cousin, it could even be *fun*.

Most of the early online dating sites focused on helping single people meet someone who might turn out to be "the one." And then, in 2002, along came Ashley Madison, a site for people who already had a partner, and whose sole purpose was to help people have a fling on the sly.

"But why?" you ask (or do you?). Well, it came down to the data. The founder of Ashley Madison read that thirty percent of people on Match.com who were looking for a partner were already in a committed relationship. Why not offer them a place where they could cheat more "honestly?" Launched originally in Canada, the service sought to link up bored, taken-for-granted, or revenge-seeking spouses who were willing to gamble with their relationships for the thrill of having a secret affair.

Before online dating, cheating was an almost comical endeavor—office trysts, spontaneous escapades in the backseats of dubious vehicles, and those ever-clichéd affairs with your spouse's best friend. Oh, the drama! Then there was the good ol' drunken rendezvous at the local dive bar, with someone whose last name you'd probably never learn.

Then, in swept the internet, throwing shade and sunlight in equal measure. Suddenly, affairs got an upgrade! No more awkward, accidental run-ins at the grocery store or hastily deleted text messages—affairs evolved from messy improvisations into meticulously planned escapades. Want discretion with a side of compatibility? Done! Rather than a sloppy one-night stand, love affairs (if you could still call them that) transformed into long-term rendezvous.

By this time, the use of online networks was already exploding. Then came the iPhone, and that changed... well, everything. You don't need me to explain how important smartphones are in today's culture—how "to tinder" has become as common-place a verb as "to google." Our ability to flirt, find dates, stalk exes, and hook up with strangers would never be the same.

With apps like Tinder leading the charge, Ashley Madison almost feels like the online dating scene's innocent predecessor—kindergarten, meet college. Now, instead of resorting to the charm of newspaper classifieds or that serendipitous bar meet-cute, we're living in the age of the mighty swipe! Just a quick flick of your finger, and voilà, your next adventure awaits.

Avid Life Media got in on the action early and bought a number of online dating platforms. Alongside Ashley Madison, these included HotOrNot, of *The Social Network* fame—the site that helped inspire the creation of Facebook.

At that point, there were no truly global dating sites. Platforms like Match.com and eHarmony operated in multiple countries, but under different names and branding. After talking with some friends in Germany who had launched highly successful dating sites there, and with me having invested in Avid Life Media a couple of years prior, I decided I wanted to have a more hands-on role with Ashley Madison. "We need to take this international," I said. And that's exactly what we did.

Some of my friends were understandably skeptical. "Are you sure about this venture?" Tommy asked me over dinner one night. "It's ... unconventional, to say the least."

I leaned forward over the table. "Tommy, the future of connection is online. The days of blind dates and nightclub flings are phasing out. And the internet ... it's the Wild West. But think about it: while many platforms cater to specific cultures or regions, basic human desires, they're universal."

"But Tino," Tommy interjected, "this site is about ... affairs! How can you align with that, morally?"

I took a deep breath, recalling the myriad reactions and challenges I'd already received from others. "Tommy, the platform may facilitate, but it doesn't instigate. And while it's labeled as a site for infidelity, many on there are just seeking a connection, whether they're single or otherwise. It's less about the act and more about the underlying reasons."

Tommy seemed unsatisfied. "You're diving headfirst into a domain you don't even fully grasp."

I looked at him, nodding. I had had conversations like this before. "I know, I have no idea about SEO, SEM, bounce rate."

Tommy took a big sip of his wine. "You're a fish out of water, Tino."

Chuckling, I retorted, "I might not know what bounce rate means today, but that's not the game I'm playing. It's about the bigger picture. We've got some of the best minds on board. I don't need to know every fancy term. I need to understand people, desire, connection."

Our conversation ebbed and flowed with the night, touching on ethics, business acumen, and the future of the digital age. Tommy pushed back, questioned, and even doubted, but beneath it all, there was a sense of intrigue.

Raising my glass, I concluded, "To new ventures, challenges, and understanding the ever-evolving human heart."

Tommy, after a moment's hesitation, clinked his glass against mine.

The years I spent working with Avid were enlightening. Over the years, I've had the privilege of being invited on to numerous TV shows, radio programs, and podcasts to share my insights on relationships, the complexities of infidelity, the reasons for divorce, and the other intricate dynamics of human connections.

In 2012, with a head full of memories, I left the online dating industry. But as I ventured into newer avenues, a part of me always lingered back in those hallways. I had garnered data from millions, peeling back layers of human emotion, even though I was moving on, there was a whisper in my head that my journey to understand the vital elements of enduring love was incomplete.

It just didn't seem right. People were looking for something, and I had learned so much about why they felt there was something missing, and what it was that they were missing. I felt somewhat helpless, yet I knew I had to act. I just wasn't clear at that time what it was that I wanted to do, or had to do.

One day, years later, I had an epiphany that suddenly and drastically altered my way of thinking about relationships. My revelation was this: all of these relationships started out in a positive way. These couples were all in love—or at least they had been, once. And in the majority of these relationships, the partners still loved each other. But somehow, that had stopped being enough.

I've often hummed along to "Escape (The Piña Colada Song)" by Rupert Holmes. Take a moment, look up the song, and really listen to the lyrics. It's a catchy tune, but have you ever really listened to the words?

Think about it: a man, feeling a little lost in the familiar tune of his relationship, dances toward the unknown beats of a personal ad. And just when you think you've predicted the next note, there's a twist. The mysterious voice on the other side? It's his own partner. It makes me wonder: are we all just humming along, missing the details that once made our hearts skip a beat?

It's not just a question of what people are looking for, but also why they are looking to find it outside of their own relationship. How has everything gotten so fogged up in their partnership that these people—once and, often, still in love—can no longer find each other? How can they unfog this situation?

It's not a matter of glossing things over—this is too deep for that. Think of a rusty metal pole—not a very romantic image, but bear with me. If you put a coat of paint on the outside of the pole, it will look shiny and nice. But the paint won't stick for long. If you really want to repair the pole, you need to grind the rust away, clean the pole, put on primer, and then add fresh paint.

The same applies to our lives. On the outside, things may seem great, and you can address the exterior and apply some paint, but for how long? Under the surface, there may be rust. And only if the rust is taken off and the primer is put on can we fix it so it lasts. Anything else makes no sense.

I remember speaking with my friend Andreas when all of this was crystallizing for me. Our friendship had been built on deep conversations, and this meeting was no different.

It was an October afternoon in 2020, the warmth of the sun muted by the strange stillness of the streets. It was one of those hesitant reopenings during Covid—restaurants barely populated, the staff wearing masks, their eyes revealing the mix of hope and fear that everyone felt. Tables, normally buzzing with laughter and conversation, were spaced awkwardly apart, a testament to a new world order.

There was an undeniable comfort in seeing a familiar face in unfamiliar times, yet my recent experiences had instilled in me a sense of reflection, one I couldn't shake.

"I've been thinking a lot since the ICU," I told him. "I was too selfish, Andreas. I let myself be guided—misguided—by the wrong values, the wrong beliefs. I chased success without truly understanding its meaning."

There was a moment of silence before Andreas replied. "Sometimes, it takes a jolt to set the compass straight," he said.

I nodded. "All those years in internet dating, seeing the underlying causes of infidelity and broken relationships, made me understand the vast difference between happiness and fulfillment. And now, I want to do something about it. I'm restructuring everything—my life, my priorities. I have to build the Dietrich Institute. We need to go out there and help people save their relationships, one at a time."

Andreas smiled. "You've always had an intuitive understanding of relationships, and people in general. And you've always been a man of action. I've seen you mentor, guide, and coach countless individuals. It's time to channel all that knowledge and expertise into something profound."

Our conversation deepened, exploring the layers of relationships. I shared my epiphanies, including the one that had shaken my core beliefs: an affair is not the root cause of a strained relationship, but a mere symptom. Akin to painting over rust, what some relationships have is a temporary façade that hides, not heals. True healing necessitates removing the rust, laying a primer of understanding, and repainting with love and care.

As we spoke, I couldn't help but notice Andreas's growing impatience with our waitress, who seemed overwhelmed.

Sensing an opportunity, I said, "Remember nobility? It's not about the grandeur of kings and queens. It's about understanding, compassion." Gesturing toward the waitress, I continued, "With the world wrestling with a pandemic, imagine her apprehension. What if the café closes again? What if there's another wave?"

Andreas's demeanor softened. When our bill arrived, we left a generous tip, symbolizing our shared moment of compassion and understanding.

The evening was a journey through time, emotions, and life's philosophies. As I headed home, it felt like I was emerging from a fog, understanding more clearly than ever that our relationships and the problems within them aren't about the "what," but the "why." The seeds of the Dietrich Institute were sown.

It's all about relationships

The most important aspect of our lives is our relationships. I'm not just talking about relationships with partners, but with family members, with friends, with business associates and work colleagues, with the people in your digital tribes and local community, with everyone in your life.

Remember the happiness study Tommy mentioned in the introduction to this book? The Harvard Study of Adult Development commenced in 1938, dedicated to discovering what elements truly make people thrive.[9] The results have been a revelation: it is not health, fame, or fortune that foster happiness in and with one's life, but close relationships. It is the quality and strength of our relationships that dictate whether we flourish. Relationships are essential to our well-being, and so is purpose.

When I was lying in that ICU bed, I knew that this could not be all there was. There had to be more. What was my purpose?

I couldn't think about this question without thinking about my family, about the relationships we all have at home, and about how not everyone has a loving home to grow up in and family values to nurture them. I've witnessed how much suffering there is, the neglect in long-term relationships, the broken homes. People in such situations have a hard time building self-belief; they struggle to act as a guiding light for those who need guidance most—our children, the foundation of our life and our future.

Purpose is about more than what you do, it is about why you do it—being conscious when it comes to your choices, since these inform your challenges. The Dietrich Institute grew from these seeds of understanding. Our purpose is to help people have the strongest relationships they can, including with themselves. To this end, everyone involved in the

---

9   Mineo, L. "Good genes are nice, but joy is better." *The Harvard Gazette*, April 2017. Accessed online 30 August 2023. https://news.harvard.edu/gazette/story/2017/04/over-nearly-80-years-harvard-study-has-been-showing-how-to-live-a-healthy-and-happy-life/

institute's conception holds three core pillars in common, essential in everything we do: Clarity, Consciousness, and Compassion.

Clarity, consciousness, and compassion in action

The three pillars at the heart of the Dietrich Institute are essential for guiding our relationships, in all areas of life. This includes the relationship we have with ourselves, a connection we sometimes forget about and too often neglect. (You could even consider it the most important relationship—after all, you can't divorce yourself!)

Clarity forms the foundation—without it, we wander aimlessly, lost amidst the fog of uncertainties and distractions that life often presents. It's through deep self-reflection and gaining insights into our thoughts, beliefs, and behaviors, that we can develop self-awareness and understanding.

Consciousness is the window to awareness. It ensures that we're not merely existing, but living with the purpose, intention, and understanding that come from clarity. It means being present in each and every moment. This is how we cultivate a sense of interconnectedness and oneness with the world around us. We need to recognize that we are part of a larger whole and act with unity.

Then there's Compassion—or, in broader terms, Nobility. It's not about titles or regal airs, but practical action, always motivated by a higher purpose.

Understanding the right course comes from nurturing qualities such as integrity, empathy, and kindness. Embracing this "compassionate" concept of nobility means practicing ethical conduct consistently across all areas of life. It speaks of a life where compassion isn't just a value, but an active practice, echoing in every decision and action.

When contemplating these pillars, it's crucial to recognize that our external environment and the choices we make have a profound impact on our lives, and that the challenges we face are determined by those choices.

Let's examine this idea more closely. Our external environment is more than just a backdrop; it actively shapes and molds us, weaving its way deep into our psyche. It establishes values, instills beliefs, and sets forth rules that we often unknowingly adopt in our lives. While these inherited guidelines sometimes align harmoniously with our internal compass, there are times they diverge, leading us astray from our true essence and purpose. These external standards can become misleading, causing internal conflicts when they don't resonate with our authentic selves.

The choices we make in response to both these external pressures and our internal beliefs define our path. Every decision, no matter how minor it might seem, sets off a ripple of consequences. The challenges we encounter are not merely random occurrences, they are a direct reflection of our past choices. It's akin to sowing seeds—the kind we choose to plant determines the harvest we reap. So understanding the intricate interplay between our external influences and our personal choices is crucial. It's not merely about reacting to life, but consciously choosing actions that resonate with our inner truths, and navigating challenges with purpose and understanding.

Each step of the way, in each and every situation, you have to ask yourself a set of questions. In the circumstances in which I find myself, what does being clear mean for me? What does clarity look like here? How can I communicate this? What does being conscious entail, given what's going on? What elements do I need to be aware of—what do I need to understand?

What decisions you make—how you behave—is tied to your values. Given what you believe in, what actions do you need to take to be true to yourself?

Look for the little red shoes

My mom had a wonderful friend called Anna. Anna was an older lady who had lost her husband and her son. She lived to a hundred and two, but her son was taken from her by AIDS when he was in his forties. Life had dealt her harsh cards, yet somehow she was the most wonderful, life-embracing person I've ever known. She enjoyed life like no one else. She was a bright light in a dark room, the brightest candle you can imagine.

My daughter, Calyssa, was four or five years old when she met Anna, and I'll never forget the old woman complimenting my little daughter on her red shoes. Any time after that, when my daughter and I spoke to my mom and Anna, when they went for a coffee and we FaceTimed, Anna would say, "Do you still have those beautiful red shoes?" It always made my daughter laugh.

Anna was always smiling, grateful to be alive, positive and joyful. After she passed, my mom and I would turn to each other in dark moments just to remind ourselves that such a shining light existed. "Remember Anna?" we'd ask, "Remember Anna?" And we would immediately gain perspective on whatever we were dealing with.

We meet many people on our journey through this world, and it's the ones like Anna we need to bring into our hearts and manifest in our lives—those who call out the positive and frame life around lifting others up, rather than the opposite. Unfortunately, the opposite is something we're all too familiar with.

Let's be honest, sometimes it can seem like we're surrounded by assholes—and I'm not going to pretend I haven't been one myself in the past. We've all met the guy who cuts you off on the road, who shoves past you convinced their life is more busy and important than your own, who turns a simple trip to the supermarket into a day-ruining experience by being rude. These people stick out, and they have the ability to infect your day. Maybe you start driving home, and don't let someone pull out in front of you on your way back. Maybe you snap at your partner when you get back in the door, and get impatient with your kids.

An episode with my son comes to mind here. I remember the humid air of Hong Kong clinging to our skin as we navigated the bustling streets, the city's iconic skyline a towering backdrop. Making our way to the gleaming, ultramodern train station, a structure straight out of a sci-fi movie, Corbinian's eyes were wide with wonder. It was his eighteenth birthday gift, a trip with his old man to a city he had dreamt about for years, and here we were, about to embark on a journey to Shenzhen on the high-speed train.

The excitement was palpable, but it was juxtaposed with the mad rush of the Hong Kong crowds, each individual engrossed in their own universe, rushing to and fro. As we stood in line, waiting to board the train, the thrum of conversations around us blended into a rhythmic city lullaby.

Suddenly, like a gust of wind, a man hurtled past us, his suitcase smacking into Corbinian's leg as he zoomed by. There was no acknowledgment, no apology—just the fleeting sight of his back as he disappeared into the crowd, clearly in a race against time. My son's face flushed red, the shock giving way to anger.

"Hey you!" he shouted, frustration evident in his voice. "Can't you watch out?"

I watched as Corbinian's emotions surged, a tidal wave of indignation. I recalled my younger self, who would have most certainly reacted in the same hot-blooded way. But time has a way of tempering our reactions, teaching us to see things from a broader perspective.

Placing a hand on his shoulder, I pulled him aside, ensuring we weren't causing any obstruction. "Corbinian," I began, my voice calm and steady, "I understand how you feel. It's maddening, especially when people seem so careless. But you've got to understand, everyone has their own story. What if he just got a distressing call and was rushing back? We can't know his story, son."

He looked at me, his brow furrowed, processing my words.

"But he should've at least apologized," he muttered.

I smiled gently. "True. But think about this—the few seconds where his thoughtlessness has interrupted our day aren't worth carrying minutes, or even hours, of agitation afterward. Our journey here is fleeting, so why let these brief moments rob us of our peace?"

The buzzing station continued its animated dance around us. Corbinian nodded, taking a deep breath and exhaling slowly. "I guess you're right, Dad."

I pulled him into a hug. "This is just a small blip in our adventure. Let's focus on the memories we're making."

With that, we boarded the train, leaving behind the frenzied station and looking forward to the journey ahead.

Think about this: what if, instead of focusing on the actions of a few, when we went into situations we looked only for the little red shoes? What if we went out of our way to compliment someone, even just smile at them in the supermarket? What could that achieve? Maybe they would take that little lift home with them, into their lives. Maybe they'd even pass it on.

This is why I have a motto: "One less asshole."

If enough people make a conscious decision to approach things differently, we could spread compassion rather than small-mindedness, rather than meanness. Every week, we could end up with one less person out there ruining someone's day, simply because they were treated kindly one day and passed that on instead. A ripple effect.

Next time you're in the supermarket, doing the chores, try this experiment. Be on the lookout for something that's positive, something that's beautiful, something that you will remember. Smile at a stranger and pay them a compliment.

Remember Anna. And look for the little red shoes.

EMBRACING
TRUE COMPASSION

Learning to listen

Some people, like Anna, always stay with you. They stick in your mind because of their compassion, their approach to life, and how they made you feel.

The importance of examining how people make you feel and, in turn, how *you* make people feel cannot be overstated. It's about emotional intelligence—about being really clear on how we affect other people and why. This is where consciousness comes into the equation. We have a choice about how to act and how to treat people. Complimenting others isn't an empty act—it means that you're really present with a person, learning what's important to them (and perhaps overlooked by others), and calling it out in the open. It's about good communication, and that starts with listening.

Someone who always listened to me deeply was my Uncle Misha. He was actually my great-uncle, one of my grandmother's two brothers. When he was a child, he fell down the stairs and broke his back. He recovered and was able to walk again, but not very well. He moved very slowly, and he was left with a hunchback from the collapse of his vertebra. Yet I never met anyone who could charm women like him—he was full of charisma, so much character.

I first met him in the spring of 1983, when my father and I went to look at a boarding school. We went to visit him in his apartment, and my dad impressed upon me the need to make a good impression.

"Please behave," he stressed. "When he opens the door and looks at you, say hello and greet him properly."

I could tell that Misha meant a lot to my father, and that he held him in the greatest respect. I was immediately nervous. Who was going to open the door?

The door opened a little bit, then all the way. A man with small glasses peeked out like a little mouse. He looked at us standing on his doorstep, then looked directly at me.

"You can come in," he said.

My dad moved forward, but then Misha pulled me inside alone and closed the door behind me. Now I was really afraid.

"*Oh God,*" I thought. "*What do I do? What if I do something wrong? What if I say something wrong?*"

He sat me down and immediately put me at ease. He really cared why I was there that day, and he wanted to talk to me away from my father, so I'd feel like I could be honest, to say what I was really thinking.

"Do you want to go to this boarding school?" he asked. "Is it something you want for yourself?"

"I don't know," I said.

He looked at me. "Tell me why."

He really listened to me, made me feel like a grown-up. He even pulled out a couple of tiny silver cups and poured me a small drink.

We were close from that time on, and I went to visit him many times, always learning something new. But the lesson that stands out above all is how you can make someone feel by truly listening to them, and caring about what they say.

When he was dying, I went to see him in the hospital. "How is he feeling?" I asked the nurse on duty.

She gave me a sad look. "He is very weak." She was about to leave the room as I was entering it, but she looked back at me. "He is really one of the most amazing men I've ever met."

I looked at her questioningly, and she gave me the most beautiful smile.

"I just had my hair done at the hairdresser," she said, "and this morning I came into his room. He's in pain, can barely speak, but the first thing he says to me is how wonderful my hair looks today. How it's different to when he saw me last."

I nodded, smiling myself.

"I wish my husband would recognize things like that," she continued, "me and my new hair." She looked back into the room at my great-uncle. "He is full of compassion. You can tell. His compliment made my day. He knew it would mean a lot to me. He's dying." She looked at me kindly. "He's getting weaker. Yet he cares about making my day."

That's what he was like, my great-uncle Misha. So I challenge you again to take up the compliment experiment—to nurture compassion, so we can see how much we can pass along. Let's make the world brighter and brighter, by listening, by caring, one compliment at a time. This is how we make the world a better place.

What role does compassion play in your life? When was the last time someone truly listened to you—and you truly listened to another? My time in the online dating industry taught me so much about human connection and what we need to flourish. It is kindness and empathy—nobility—that we need to cultivate in our lives for our relationships to thrive. The beacon of compassion is a torch that can be lit from one person to another, setting the whole world ablaze.

5

CHANGING PERSPECTIVE

W HEN YOU'RE LOST in a maze of streets at the heart of a labyrinthine metropolis, it's easy to feel like you'll never find your way. There are twists and turns and dead ends. You may double back on yourself by mistake, or get stuck in a one-way system that means you go in a circle. You may end up at the base of a landmark more than once and despair of getting where you want to go.

But what happens if you get out of the maze? Imagine riding an elevator to the top of a skyscraper and standing at the very top—the tallest building in the city. Suddenly, you can see the streets, the landmarks, the suburbs all stretching out beneath you. You understand the route you could take to get to your destination.

The beacon of perspective is a wayfinder that provides guidance and support. It illuminates the path if the route is unclear, when you reach a crossroads, or should the way become blocked. It is a profound power we each hold—to redefine our view of the world and, in doing so, to reimagine the trajectory of our journey. Sometimes it takes trauma, tragedy, and suffering to prompt such reimagining, and urge us to seek meaning and seize the day. A miscarriage, a near-death epiphany—these landmarks encouraged me to change the way I looked at things. How can we cultivate a healthy mind as well as a healthy body? What is happiness, and why are we bent on pursuing it as though it's a chase? What can we do to heal from old wounds?

As we traverse this chapter, we'll step away from the city's bustling streets, journeying instead through the complex chambers of the soul, chasing such pure, resonant moments of clarity. Our story, in all its complexity, is largely influenced by how we choose to see it. A shift in perspective is a conscious choice to view things differently, and this is a path to healing that can truly transform your life.

Finding the words

Picture a couple preparing their home, and their family, for the birth of their third child. It's a joyful time, with two very excited little boys—especially the youngest one, who can't entirely grasp the situation, why it's happening, and everything it means, but who understands he's going to become a big brother.

The parents have spent time preparing the kids for a new baby coming into the house, teaching them that there will need to be adjustment, that there will need to be gentleness with the new little one, that there will need to be quiet time when the baby is sleeping. Family shopping trips are undertaken, and the two boys pick out gifts for the newcomer, to present when the time comes.

But the time doesn't come. One day their mom doesn't feel very well. She is rushed to hospital in severe pain. The ultrasound they perform reveals no heartbeat.

THIS WAS not our only experience of miscarriage, but it was the first where my wife Silke and I had to explain to two little boys that there was no baby coming after all. I'll never forget how my younger son, Caspar, only about three years old, was so excited to be an older brother, and so confused when we told him things had changed. He couldn't really understand, being too young.

Corbinian was about five at the time. Heartbreakingly, he wanted to know if he'd done something wrong—if the baby didn't like him, and so had chosen not to come.

It was tough to stay calm, to explain everything in the best possible way, while also dealing with my own emotions.

Eventually, my boys got a little sister. But I will never forget the journey that led to our family being complete. One of my biggest inspirations for expanding my business aims came from this very personal experience.

When you're single, everyone asks when you're going to get married, and when you're married, everyone asks when you're going to have kids. But here we were, trying to do just that, and it felt like no one knew quite how to talk to us about our loss. No one seemed to recognize the toll it had taken on our mental health, and the influence that it had on our relationship.

It all started to crystallize for me. No aspect of ourselves or our relationships exists in isolation. We have to invest in our health and well-being at every level—physical, mental, emotional—in order to be truly present for our loved ones, and to have the relationships we crave. Ultimately, this is one of the realizations that led me to create the Dietrich Institute, so that I could help people take an integrated approach to enriching their lives as well as their relationships.

When the universe repeats itself

My fight with Covid in the ICU wasn't the first time I was made to contemplate the end being nigh. I'd been faced with the idea of my own death before.

In the spring of 2015, I remember waiting impatiently for my wife to pick me up from our house. She had just dropped our daughter at school. My pain was getting worse minute by minute, and I could barely crawl into the car. She drove up to the emergency room of Baptist Hospital in Miami, where I was immediately given some heavy-duty medication against the pain.

I'd had kidney stones before, so I was pretty sure I had won the stone lottery again. But when the doctor came back from running some tests, she said they'd seen something unusual, related to my liver. It made her decide to send me for an MRI. I was pumped full of medication, and I'd been going through so much it just seemed like one more thing. I just added it to the list.

When it was time for the results and I faced the doctor again, I could tell something was very wrong.

"It's liver cancer," she told me.

I couldn't wrap my head around the diagnosis. I was in the States, and meant to be back in Germany, so I took all the results back over there and contacted my doctor. I had been a patient of his years, and when I told him it was urgent, he made time to see me right after I landed.

He sat across from me, looking through the material I'd brought.

"Whoa," he said. Which is not something you want to hear from your doctor.

"Why? What?" I said. "What's going on? So it's cancer? It's definitely cancer?"

He looked thoughtful. "I actually don't think it's cancer."

I tried to process this. "But if it is? What does that mean?"

"If this *is* liver cancer," he stressed, "there's not a lot we can do. Liver cancer is very problematic." He studied my face. "Let's run some more tests. Let's hope it's not, and try to rule it out."

"But what if?" I said, a stuck record. "What if?"

He saw how badly I needed an answer. "If it *were* cancer we're seeing right here, you'd have anywhere between three to six months."

I left his office a mess. I was seriously scared.

Wait, he says it might not be cancer, I said to myself.

But I answered myself as well. *Maybe that's what they do with everybody. They don't tell them it's cancer right away, in case they freak out and go jump off a balcony.*

My wife called me. "What did he say?"

I spiraled again. What should I tell her? That he said he didn't actually think it was cancer, even though I'd already been told it was cancer—but if it was, then I might only have a matter of months to live?

I remember sitting on a park bench and staring out across the lake. *What if? What if? What the fuck?*

"It can't be," I said to myself. "It isn't."

And it wasn't. But what a moment.

Perhaps that's when I was meant to first ask myself, "If this is the end, how do I feel? Is this everything I wanted before I go? Is this everything I wanted to be?"

But I didn't. I didn't receive the message from the universe. I wasn't listening closely enough. I needed more than that close call being a false call.

A few short years later, Covid struck.

"Hey," life was telling me. "You've had so many opportunities to understand the message. Here's the last one. Apparently you're not listening, so let me spell it out for you."

There are two things I remember hearing very clearly while I was in the ICU that summer of 2020. One was the "code blue" announcement that came over the speakers when someone's heart stopped. And the other was the *Rocky* theme song.

I heard the latter from time to time, but I thought I was dreaming. I had to ask the nurse what was going on.

"What's the *Rocky* music for?" I asked.

She smiled. "Every time someone leaves here with Covid and can go back home, we play the music when we push them out of hospital."

Unfortunately, it was the code blue I heard more often. It must have been only my first or second night in there when the guy in the bed next to me died. I had been listening to him coughing since I got in there, but that morning it was quiet.

"What happened?" I asked the nurse.

"He passed away," she said, and started to cry.

Not long after, I got the phone call from the pastor.

This can't be it, I thought. *It can't be.*

But then I started to unpack it. Remember how I spoke of Claus in the introduction? He was my oldest friend; I had known him since kindergarten, and he was my daughter's godfather. I was devastated that Claus, only a year older than me, had recently died of Covid, leaving behind two boys about the same age as my sons. What if this was it for me?

No, I thought as I lay there. *This can't be over.*

I couldn't figure it out, but I had something left to do. There was something missing. I couldn't possibly go, leaving this world the way things were.

All my life I'd pursued some version of happiness as though it was a drug. I'd spent my life chasing false happiness, defined by other people's values and beliefs and rules. And I suddenly felt pretty shallow.

I had a great life. A wonderful wife. Three great kids. I'd had ups and downs, but I'd known more success than failure. I knew without a doubt, though, that I had let myself down.

If I get out of here, I thought, *I'll make up for it. I'll change things. I'll stop wasting time. I'll live with purpose. I'll find meaning.*

I realized straight away that I didn't even know what that meant—just that it was missing. I needed to understand my purpose, identify my meaning.

When I get out of here, I thought, *that's what I'll do.*

I repeated it like a mantra: *So I've got to get out of here. I've got to get out of here.*

A healthy mind

My health has come up quite a bit in this book so far, and after a lot of rehabilitation and recovery, I've obviously come out believing how important it is to look after your body. But I want to stress how vitally important it is to take care of your mind as well. We all know by now that they are connected, but it's equally obvious that we feed them in different ways.

My daughter Calyssa is a pescatarian who is very mindful about what she eats, all the elements she takes and puts in her body. Sound familiar?

We all talk so much about what to eat and what not to eat, and that's great. But why don't we spend equal time talking about what to think and what not to think? We should focus on taking on board thoughts that are good for us too. It's a different kind of nutrition, but it's beyond important for our whole selves.

We need to apply the same filter and consciousness to our mind that we do to our physical health. You want to exercise because you don't want excess fat in your body? Great! But what about exercising your mind? You wouldn't choose only one part of your body to exercise, would you—say, your right arm, ignoring everything else? Nobody does that. You want a whole physique.

All I'm saying is, we need to consider our mind as part of this picture of "wholeness." We have to get clear about what we want to feed our whole selves.

The pursuit of happiness

Getting through life, getting to the top, is often described as a race—a rat race. We're brought up being told we better get running, and we run and run and don't stop. But what are we chasing? And what happens once we cross the finish line? What even is the finish line—what are we racing for?

Like so many others, in the beginning I was chasing this idea of "happiness." But what we think is happiness is an illusion. It's not a destination we can get to. You don't get handed happiness if you win the race. It's especially confusing these days, because we're surrounded by images of fake happiness. In the media, on social media, there in our faces on our phones, on the internet twenty-four hours a day, we're bombarded with people showing us what they've got, what they've achieved, how happy they are—whether they actually feel happy or not.

Have you heard the expression, "With the money we don't have, we buy the things we can't afford, to impress the people we don't like?" The idea was made famous in the movie *Fight Club*, and is originally attributed to Robert Quillen talking about Americanism, but I came across it when studying the life of the business tycoon Aristotle Onassis. The point is, money is made out to be this key performance indicator of success—the happiness KPI. It makes people feel bad because they don't have what these other people have, and they're told it's what would make them happy; it paints a picture of a blissful life. But it's a false picture. It doesn't just leave out the bad bits—the challenges, the struggles—it leaves out the meaningful parts; the parts that make life worth living.

We need to be conscious of all this. The true blissful life that we're looking for is only possible if we have clarity.

A disclaimer here: I'm not saying if we have clarity, we are guaranteed a blissful life. What I'm saying is that the chance to have a true, blissful life without having clarity is slim. It's almost like expecting to win the lottery without the right six numbers—it doesn't make sense. "Oh, I only had five." Well, then you didn't win the lottery. You can't hit the jackpot without every single number right. And that's clarity. Five numbers are five numbers—it's not bad, don't get me wrong. Many people would take it; they'd even take four numbers. But you want to hit the jackpot? You've got to have clarity.

Clarity to me is the basis of everything. If you have no clarity, then you have no perspective, you have no purpose, you have no understanding, you have no self-love, you have no relationships, because everything is unclear. Only if you have clarity can you gain perspective and actually make sense of things.

TRUE HAPPINESS IS A CHOICE   TRUE WORRY IS A CHOICE

OUR TRUE CHOICE

My friend Kirsten Kuhnert, known as Kiki—an established coach, the founder and president of the not-for-profit organization Dolphin Aid, and author of the book *Every Day a Little Miracle*—always says, "Happiness is a choice." Like the famous saying, "When life gives you lemons, make lemonade," it's a very simple concept, but it holds a world of truth. We need to choose how we react to things. If we look at things from a different perspective, we'll be able to overcome hurdles and make those lemons into something that, at the very least, is less bitter to swallow. If we allow the things that happen around us to dictate how we should feel, we become the victims of our own thoughts.

We wake up in the morning, and if there's something wrong, we say we've picked up the flu, we've got the symptoms, we're coughing and stuffed up and feel terrible, and then we immediately react badly. "Oh no! But I'm meant to be doing this and that. I'm meant to be traveling over there. Now I can't!"

But every other morning, when we wake up without the flu, are we grateful? Do we react in the opposite way? "Oh wow, thanks body! I'm not sick today. I feel great!"

Which way makes you happier, do you think? We should cherish every day. We should be grateful, not wait until good things are taken away, or we have days left to live, and then start thinking, "I wish, I wish..." Gratitude is the perspective we should cultivate right now for everything we already have.

My old boss and good friend Rolf used to say, "Happiness is a function of accepting what is." If you can accept the present, you can be happy. When Kiki says, "Happiness is a choice," that is what she means.

As I've said throughout this book, we're victims of our conditioning, of how society has shaped us. But we can choose not to be.

The way we grew up literally shapes how we see things. Take the color blue—it's been argued the way we see it is a modern development. In the past, it's possible that the concept of the color blue didn't exist; even today, people from certain cultures may not see it the same as we do in the West.[10]

Unraveling what's right and wrong is like attempting to pair socks in a dark laundry room. From the get-go, we're handed a pile of "socks"—values, beliefs, rules—which aren't always our preferred style. As we grow, we try to sort and match these pairs, making alterations here and there. But sometimes we end up stuck with mismatched pairs, as we adhere strictly to these taught "sock-sorting rules." We don't question; we make assumptions. What's worse, we let others—friends, society, social media—dictate our sock-matching technique. We start wearing mismatched pairs just because someone told us it's trendy. This messes up our sock drawer. And if everyone else also has mismatched socks, nobody realizes they're stepping out in odd socks. It's the definition of lacking clarity—of being fogged up.

The thing to remember is, *you're in charge of your sock drawer*. Your happiness depends on your choices. It's not about fixing people; it's about shifting their perspective.

As Kiki suggests, take a piece of art. When you look at a painting or a sculpture, you can look at it from different angles. You can stand right in front of it, or you can stand to the left or right of it; you can sit below and

---

10 Carpineti, A. "Did Ancient People Really Not See the Color Blue?" *IFL Science*, August 2020. Accessed online 6 August 2023. https://www. iflscience.com/did-ancient-people-really-not-see-the-color-blue-51837

look up at it, or you can look down on it. Depending on what position you are looking from, things will look different—but it's the same painting, the same sculpture.

That's what we need to do with ourselves. We need to look at our life from different perspectives. This is how we gain clarity. This is how we can move about and see how these guiding principles can make a difference in our lives.

It's our choices that determine our challenges. The more conscious the choices we make, the higher the chance the challenges we face become more than just obstacles—they become opportunities for growth. And that is how we shift our perspective in terms of what we see. That is when we can appreciate life happening *for* us, rather than to us.

Healing from old wounds

A few years back, finding ourselves in the same city for different reasons, an old friend and I sat down for a catch-up. I'd known her for a long time: a highly accomplished woman who had achieved lots of success in both her professional and personal life, she had many wonderful qualities, and she'd always seemed like she would be an ideal partner for someone. Yet she'd been single for many years.

I couldn't help but wonder why that was. On this particular evening, I decided to ask her about it. I phrased my question as delicately as possible, but she didn't answer right away—and for a second, I thought I was about to get her drink thrown in my face.

When her response finally came, it caught me off guard—I think it was more honest than I was expecting.

"I don't trust men," she said.

"Why not?" I asked.

She took a sip of her wine, and, judging from the amount of liquid that disappeared from her glass, I could tell that my question had a complicated answer.

"In my last serious relationship, my boyfriend cheated on me," she began. "When I caught him, we talked it all out, and I thought that we had smoothed things over. But a few months later, he went right back to the other woman. Actually, I don't know if he ever stopped seeing her in the first place."

She sighed. "So, we split up. Afterward, I started dating again right away. By some miracle, I managed to meet a few men I liked. But with all of them, after a little while, things would start to go wrong. To be honest? It was my fault."

"What do you mean?" I prompted, when she seemed to have gotten lost in thought.

"I kept finding myself overreacting to the most inconsequential things. Every time a boyfriend checked his cell phone, or wasn't available at the drop of a hat, I figured that he must be seeing someone behind my back. It got so bad that I started breaking up with people for no real reason—because I was sure it was only a matter of time before I got cheated on again."

She shrugged. "It wasn't like I didn't *want* to be in a relationship. I did, but my anxiety always got the better of me. Whenever I got close to getting what I wanted, I ended up sabotaging it."

"Sounds like you never really recovered from that first betrayal," I said.

"Exactly. Call it my tragic backstory, I guess," she replied. "I did the same thing with my most recent boyfriend, Sam. I started to notice him sneaking off into the other room to text, or going outside the house to have quick conversations on his cell phone. And I just got paranoid. It became such a source of stress to me that, one day, I decided to just move out."

"Oh no."

She grimaced and nodded. "While he was at work, I cleared out my closet, packed all of my stuff into my car, and took off for my mother's house, fifty miles away. That night, I got a text from my best friend. Know what it said? 'Hey, where you at? Me and all your friends are over here to celebrate your six-month anniversary with Sam.'"

She groaned at the memory, and took another gulp of wine.

My friend's story illustrates an all-too-common stumbling block for couples. Many of us have similar stories about a relationship from hell, the subsequent trainwreck of a breakup, and the resulting scar that never quite healed.

Did you know, for people who divorce once and remarry, the divorce rate goes up and up? One-time divorcees are more likely to divorce a second time; two-time divorcees are even more likely. The hopeful newlyweds just don't understand that while they might have left a house, tidied the drawers out, and moved on, they've taken whole drawers into the next house, the next relationship. They've taken along all the trash. You can change partners, but the problems remain the same. In a boat race, the wind is the same for all vessels; how you fare is about how you set the sail and turn the rudder. You can't blame the wind for losing the race.

Too often, we take the problems from one relationship and carry them with us into the next. This is unfair both to our partners and to ourselves. As you can see from my friend's tale of woe, it can lead to repeating patterns of conflict, and even self-sabotage.

These types of issues don't always stem from negative experiences in romantic relationships, either. Some of us have experienced abuse, neglect, manipulation, or other traumas at the hands of parents or family members. If you learn to expect this behavior from those closest to you at a young age, you might find yourself anticipating those same problems in your significant other, even if they have no intention of hurting you. It's important to realize that this kind of defensive thinking, where you feel like you constantly need to protect yourself from others, doesn't come from nowhere. It's a learned behavior that people adopt to help them cope with tough situations.

But if we don't recognize the root causes of those behaviors and take the time to process them, we can end up holding onto dysfunctional coping mechanisms and destabilizing even the best relationships. Without healing, those past traumas will infect new relationships, undermining trust and impeding intimacy. How can you open up to someone if you don't trust them? How can you be vulnerable and authentic? You'll find yourself compromising the relationship before it ever has a chance to flourish.

Have you heard of the acronym Future Events Appearing Real (FEAR)? If we allow FEAR to control our decisions, we aren't able to live for today. There's a saying, "God looks out for children, drunks, and fools." You can't be in the mountains skiing without seeing the kids going hell for leather down the slopes. It's amazing—they have no fear, they're completely in the moment. Compare this to the "responsible" adult at the top of the hill, not even a steep slope: "Oh God, that looks big. And I've got that big presentation Tuesday. I'm going to break a leg. I can't go too fast or I'll fall. The company will fail." That's the person who starts to ski and immediately breaks a leg, not the little kid whizzing down the mountain focusing on what's in front of them.

So now we have an injured businessman, watching more happy-go-lucky people ski down the mountain with ease. "Why me?" they ask. "Why always me?"

They've programmed themselves to break their leg, really. They're sending out the wrong message to the universe: focusing on the things they don't want, rather than the things they do.

We want life to happen *for* us, not *to* us. Rather than regretting what's come before and fearing what's to come, we need to live in the present (it's a gift!) and enjoy what is happening right now. We have to learn from our mistakes and bad experiences, but we mustn't let FEAR dictate how we live our life, as we will miss the opportunities that life presents to change the status quo.

Investing the time and energy to find peace and attain resolution is a vital step before beginning a new relationship. When that doesn't happen, people often find themselves in a new relationship that's essentially a rerun of the one they just got out of. Not a fun rerun, either—we're talking season eight *Game of Thrones* here.

Every friendship group has one of these people. The other friends watch from afar as they follow the same destructive pattern ad nauseum. (And if you can't think of who that person is in your friendship group . . . well, I hate to be the bearer of bad news.)

It can be frustrating and disheartening to watch the same old thing play out, *again*. "I can't believe they're dating him. He's just like so-and-so, except he's even worse. Why are they doing this?"

They're doing it because they're fogged up. They haven't healed from the original traumatic relationship, and they don't have clarity. Consciously or unconsciously, they're attracting the same type of partner, the same type of relationship, as the one they had before. This leads to reliving all of the unresolved problems that cropped up in the first go-round. But this is not how healing takes place.

Let's be honest, we all have baggage. Everyone we care for deeply leaves a mark on us. Even if we don't stay together forever, all of our relationships affect who we are and how we see the world. That much is inevitable. But it doesn't have to be a bad thing.

Our experiences, even painful ones, can be an opportunity to gain wisdom and help us learn more about what we want in life. When we take the time to grieve our losses, stay in tune with ourselves, and nurture a sense of inner peace, we can go into our next relationship from a place of resolution rather than pain.

My friend Paul once asked me, "You travel a lot. How does that work with your wife?"

I wasn't sure I understood him. "What do you mean, 'how does it work?'"

"Does she always know where you are?"

"Usually, more or less. Not always."

He rolled his eyes. "When I travel, I have to give my wife the name of the hotel, the room number, and all the phone numbers of the people I'm with. Then she wants to know my itinerary. We have to have before-dinner calls and after-dinner calls. It's a hassle, but I feel obligated to go along with it."

I can't say for sure, but it certainly sounds like my friend was experiencing the results of another wound that hadn't been given the time and attention it needed to heal. Is it possible that his spouse wanted to be controlling and overly demanding just for kicks and giggles? Perhaps, but it's not likely. Far more likely is that his wife, like my friend who found herself single after all those failed relationships, had been through some kind of betrayal in the past. Her requests for constant communication, which were clearly putting a strain on their marriage, probably came from a place of insecurity and fear.

It doesn't have to be that way. For people who are single, the ideal time to heal from previous relationships is before they get into a new one. For people who are already in committed partnerships and are just now coming to terms with how they might be holding on to pain from the past, the best time is right now. It will require hard work and introspection on the part of the one partner, and patience from the other. But ideally, this is what a strong partnership is all about—providing space and support to help each other grow.

TRUE TRUST VS. PERCEIVED TRUST

After all, it's about trust. Trust doesn't fall from the sky—it is built, brick by brick, step by step. However, the foundation for trust is a *capacity to trust*. If you cannot and will not trust anybody, that's what you need to work on first, or your partner will never be able to build trust with you. No matter what they do, you will always tear down what is being built up.

The path to healing can take many forms, but it starts with gaining perspective and getting clear on yourself, your path, and your purpose.

When was the last time you changed your mind about something because you got to see it in a different light? Is there anything troubling you where you might benefit from a change in perspective? The beacon of perspective challenges us to change position and see how things look. Get some distance, try a new angle, or change the lenses in your glasses—perhaps it's time for a new pair that don't get so fogged up. Having empathy for other people's suffering, experiencing our own suffering, looking back and connecting the dots— it all brings us to clarity and a new understanding.

6

A QUEST FOR
PURPOSE

IFE CAN BE a maze, a confusing collection of wrong turns and dead ends. But if we get ourselves centered, we can find a hidden oasis of calm, a secret garden where every bloom tells a story, every scent holds a memory, and where you can find a sense of direction. It is easier to reach this place with guides. An unexpected rendezvous with an Asian monk gifted me such an epiphany, and in this chapter you'll spend time with other teachers, like the insightful Kiki Kuhnert, while nudging you toward the meaning of life, which can be found in the Japanese philosophy of Ikigai.

Just as a garden thrives when tended with care, understanding our *raison d'être*, our Ikigai, requires nurturing our soul. We can get there without the transformative power of a near-death experience— we can choose to transform ourselves and give

Ikigai

A JAPANESE CONCEPT MEANING "A REASON FOR BEING"

What you
LOVE

Delight and
fullness, but
no wealth

Satisfaction,
but feeling of
uselessness

PASSION   **MISSION**

What you are
GOOD AT

Ikigai

What the
world
NEEDS

PROFESSION   **VOCATION**

Comfortable,
but feeling of
emptiness

Excitement and
complacency,
but sense of
uncertainty

What you
can be
PAID FOR

ourselves direction, heeding the path ignited by the beacon of purpose. In the end, isn't it all about tending to our internal gardens, ensuring that each choice, each breath, brings us closer to our truest self?

In the spring of 2021, I found myself amidst the urban charm of Hamburg, seeking answers to my perplexing health issues. Though I felt marginally better, my body was not cooperating the way it once did. Running, an activity I used to enjoy without a second thought, had become a strenuous task. Every few steps were punctuated by pauses, as my strength waned. The additional weight I had gained clung to me, defying my every effort to shed it. It was immensely frustrating, and the once simple joys of life felt like an arduous journey.

Hopeful for clarity, I consulted specialists at a renowned clinic in Hamburg. They plunged me into a rigorous regime of tests, casting a wide diagnostic net in an attempt to pinpoint the cause of my ailment. My anxiety grew with every test, as an intuitive part of me knew that something was amiss. The gravity of the situation became palpable when I sat across from the doctor, awaiting his analysis. As he began to elucidate their findings, derived from myriad blood samples, MRIs, and other diagnostic tools, I struggled to concentrate. His words swirled around me, blending into a cacophony of potential outcomes, as I tried to grasp the weight of the diagnosis.

"... cardiomyopathy," he repeated, and I nodded numbly.

The heart infection I had contracted due to Covid had caused damage to my heart muscle, resulting in scar-tissue formation and reduced heart function. Some of the symptoms included shortness of breath, fatigue, and swelling in the legs and ankles. Treatment would involve not only medication, but also permanent lifestyle changes. If this didn't work, then came the scary stuff: surgical interventions, implantable devices, even a heart transplant, depending on the severity of the condition and how it developed.

It was time to take some serious care of myself. It was vitally important that I work closely with my cardiologist to manage my condition and optimize my heart health. This required a lot of changes in my life, and a lot of discipline. Steadily, I combined medication with meditation, embarked on sports under supervision, took time every day to ensure I was treating my body the absolute best that I could, following the advice of medical professionals and also asking myself what I needed for my well-being.

Accepting Tech Entrepreneur of the Year award, Las Vegas, 2019. External success and recognition, while gratifying, didn't answer the deeper questions about purpose and meaning that lay ahead.

I had to be gentle with myself. I had to be kind. And every move I made contributed to my heart health—but also more than that. Holistically, my health in all areas—physical, mental, and emotional—improved and flourished.

You may have heard the analogy before, but many of us look after the health of our vehicles better than we look after ourselves. We give them oil, so they run smoothly. We check that there's enough gas in the tank before big trips. We feed them the right fuel to get us where we're going, and top them up regularly. We get them serviced and checked out and fixed when anything troubles us—we don't wait for the engine to blow up first.

Meanwhile, we don't normally go and see a specialist about our own health and well-being until something's gone really wrong. We don't make changes until we have to—until we've been scared into doing it. We don't take proper time off work until we've already burnt out. We don't appreciate our health, our mobility, until it's gone.

My own example is extreme, but there was a massive lesson there for me: don't wait. Don't wait until you're unwell to treat yourself well, to give yourself the care you deserve. Practicing self-care can help prevent issues down the road in both your body and your mind, and it can help you through them.

Once I got my health back, I knew I needed to recalibrate my compass. I committed to finding my purpose, to identifying my true north. And I began to realize that there were so many situations in my life where relationships were the key. People had played such important roles in my life, good and bad. The greatest moments were when I'd had people who helped me, with real purpose and meaning. I saw there were always people in my life who had tried to put me on the right track, but I had never followed it. I had always fallen off again.

Looking back on my life stretching out behind me, my childhood, my schooling, my business ventures, the highs and the lows, I began to join the dots. I saw those places where I could have asked myself the big questions before. All the people who had shaped me. My choices. My challenges. Things became crystal clear.

"Here's what I should do," I said to myself. "I should help people to do exactly this. To get on the right track so they don't end up like me, where it takes a life-altering moment, this epiphany in the ICU, fearing for my life, to begin to think about it."

I needed to inspire people to not pursue happiness as a feeling, but to find, identify, and pursue purpose and meaning.

Looking East

As I've mentioned, in the mid-nineties, I joined the family business. We opened offices in Southeast Asia, and I had to travel a lot. The shipping and trading we were involved in required heavy machinery and container ships. Back then, the work meant having to physically go back and forth.

To be honest, I was exhausted. It was a lot of stress, working so hard right out of college, and I wasn't managing it well. I suffered from tinnitus—a ringing in my ears—and I didn't know what to do about it until, during one trip, I reached Singapore, the hub from which to travel to Vietnam, China, and South Korea. It was where I connected with the outside world.

On this trip, even the concierge at the Ritz Carlton, my home away from home, could see I was very sick. He asked if I'd ever tried Asian medicine—what a lot of people think of as alternative medicine. He took me to meet a monk.

The monk was a very old man, dressed in black robes, carrying rickety wooden boxes. He spoke in broken English, and the concierge kindly translated so we could talk about what I needed.

The ancient man took one look at me and felt my energy. All of a sudden he was talking, while the concierge translated, giving me so much information on myself that was completely on point that I couldn't believe it. How did he know?

I ended up seeing him for acupuncture treatment. Over a series of sessions, I got stronger. My issues and illness were loosened and melted away. And I absorbed some wisdom from him as we went on, and our ability to communicate improved.

One day, he gave me some advice. He said that if you chase yourself because you don't know who you are in the moment, then you will never get to a moment where you can take a deep breath. You'll just constantly be running.

Really, it took me a while to understand, but years down the line I learned martial arts, and remembered things my physician used to say to me. I practiced martial arts not for self-defense, but in order to master my body and my emotions. And so much of it has to do with mastering breathing.

To me, breathing is one of the most underrated practices in the world. Think about it: we can survive a surprising amount of time without food, and we can even survive for some time (though much less) without water. But unless you're Tom Cruise and can hold your breath for over six minutes, you cannot survive longer than a few minutes without breathing. So how is that that while we think about what we're eating *all the time*, very few of us think every day about how best to breathe?

The Asian philosophies and practices I have embraced all support and enhance one another, and I've found them, in essence, to be as simple, as sophisticated, and as integral to my well-being as breathing. The concept of Ikigai is one such philosophy that has had a profound effect on my life.

Finding my Ikigai

Ikigai is a Japanese concept referring to something or someone giving a person a sense of purpose, or a reason to live.

Psychiatrist Mieko Kamiya, in her 1966 book *Ikigai-ni-tsuite* (*About Ikigai*), explains that the word "Ikigai" is similar to "happiness." However, it has a subtle difference, as it allows you to look forward to the future even when you feel miserable now.

Often, people mistake the idea of happiness and richness for monetary abundance, but happiness is not limited to financial success. A person can find happiness in the smallest things, like spending time with family, performing acts of service, and much more.

I believe the best way to find happiness is to first find clarity within oneself. You can never find happiness with others if you don't first experience it within yourself. Knowing yourself is essential to understanding what is important to you and where you can find your life's purpose. In this way, you are able to find fulfillment in everything you do, from work to relationships (with oneself and others). Knowing your Ikigai can help get there.

Albert Liebermann and Hector Garcia, authors of *Ikigai: The Japanese Secret to a Long and Happy Life*, have popularized this idea. Their book presents four overlapping elements, which, when combined, can help a person live a purposeful life. The elements are as follows: what you love, what the world needs, what you are good at, and what you get paid for.

What you love: this encompasses people and the things you do and experiences that give you joy in life and make you feel alive. Depending on the person, these things can range from rock climbing, to spending time with family, to playing music or other hobbies.

What the world needs: doing the things the world needs can range from performing humanitarian acts to helping a small community around you, or anything in between. Think charity work, volunteering, nursing, providing clean water, reading to the elderly, and more.

What you are good at: these are the things you particularly excel at. They can include hobbies, talents, or a skill you have learned and mastered over the years. Examples of such things include playing piano, drawing, singing, tailoring, and so on.

What you get paid for: these are the skills you possess, and people are willing to pay you to perform the service for them. Depending on a person's expertise, they can get paid for a range of different services, such as playing piano, analyzing businesses, marketing, and more.

Now, look at what happens when the different elements intersect:

When what you love overlaps with what you are good at, you discover your life's passion.

You discover your mission in life when what you love and what the world needs become one.

When what you can be paid for and what you are good at come together, you can realize your profession.

Meanwhile, your vocation is more meaningful and fulfilling when what you can be paid for and what the world needs overlap.

A person's Ikigai is usually at the center, where all four elements overlap. In other words, when a person's mission in life, passion, profession, and vocation become one, they can enjoy each part of their life to the fullest and feel their life has a purpose.

I remember, when the essence of Ikigai had crystallized for me, I explained it to my father.

It was October 2022. In the heart of Austria, the magnificent Hotel Stanglwirt unfurled before me, a symbol of Austrian grandeur. The vast lobby was bathed in the muted glow of a splendid chandelier. Polished marble floors mirrored the ambient light, and I was instantly embraced by the comforting scent of pine, the gentle notes of classical music playing in the background.

There, seated elegantly in a quiet corner, was my father. Not particularly tall, yet with an undeniable presence, his bald head gleamed under the lights. The perfect gentleman, in impeccable attire.

His eyes, always so full of life, danced with delight as he beckoned me over. "Ah, Tino!"

Approaching him, memories of our past reunions filled my thoughts.

"Dad," I began, clasping his outstretched hand, "Miami's been wonderful, but there's nothing quite like this. Being here, in the heart of Austria, with family. It's irreplaceable."

The next day I would catch up with more family members, including my father's wife, Laja, and my two half-siblings, Tatiana and Alexander.

My father's laughter, rich and hearty, echoed in the spacious lobby. "The best is yet to come! Later, you'll finally meet your nephew. Can you believe it's been so long? Laja's been talking non-stop about catching up with Silke. We want to hear all the latest about our grandkids. These gatherings, Tino, they're like a balm to the soul. It's when time stands still, and all that matters is the here and now."

As our glasses met in a cheerful clink, our conversation naturally flowed into deeper realms. I recounted my recent introspective journey, sharing how, despite professional success and familial joys, I had felt a void. My battle with Covid had been a turning point, pushing me toward my mission—imparting clarity and nurturing relationships. The principles of Ikigai had become my guiding star.

My father's eyebrows rose at mention of the term. "Ah, the age-old quest for meaning?"

"Exactly. And I've come to realize my own story is a great example of how the four elements of Ikigai can help guide someone toward finding their purpose in life."

He leaned in, a blend of pride and understanding in his gaze. "Life often throws us these curveballs, pushing us toward self-realization. It often shows us paths when we least expect it."

I nodded. "First, I realized that something was missing in my life, despite having success in business and a happy family life. This suggests that I was lacking in the 'passion' aspect of Ikigai, which refers to doing what you truly love and enjoy."

He nodded, encouraging me to go on.

"Getting sick with Covid and almost dying gave me the wake-up call that made me re-evaluate my life," I continued. "This realization helped me to identify my 'mission,' or what I'm really good at and what I can contribute to the world—which, in my case, is bringing the message of clarity into people's lives and helping them build stronger relationships."

My father sipped his drink thoughtfully. "There's nothing more important. What next?"

I counted the elements off on my fingers. "My mission is also aligned with the 'vocation' aspect of Ikigai, which refers to what the world needs and what you can be paid for. By helping others to find clarity and build stronger relationships, I am both meeting a societal need and making a career out of it."

"And the last element?" he asked, leaning forward.

I smiled. "Finally, my newfound purpose is also in alignment with the 'profession' aspect of Ikigai, which refers to what you can be paid for and what you love to do. By following my purpose, I am able to combine my passion for helping others with my desire to make a meaningful contribution to the world."

I could feel my father's joy at seeing me so certain.

"It's like a puzzle, but it's clear you've solved it," he said.

I beamed. "The four elements of Ikigai work together to form a purpose in life. By identifying what I love, what I'm good at, what the world needs, and what I can be paid for, I've been able to find a purpose that brings me great fulfillment." I clasped my hands together. "Now—let me tell you about the Dietrich Institute."

Bringing the Dietrich Institute to life

The Dietrich Institute is where my purpose finds its expression. This is where the journey has brought me. Once I had come to understand what was missing in my life, I was able to grasp that purpose moving forward and focus all my energy on empowering people, bringing the pillars of clarity, consciousness, and compassion—of nobility—into their lives.

I had found my true north, and now needed to touch as many lives as possible with my learnings around these three pillars. I needed a base from which to teach this framework, showing people what these principles can achieve and how to bring them into their lives.

And so the vision statement of the institute came into being: *A world where every home resonates with love and understanding, and every organization thrives on mutual respect and purpose, crafting a harmonious future where relationships are the cornerstone of success.*

The institute's mission? *To revolutionize relationships—from the heart of homes to the soul of businesses, by fostering personal growth, consciousness, and compassion, and breaking the cycles that limit human potential and unity.*

I stand at the heart of the Dietrich Institute as its visionary, leading its build-out as an award-winning entrepreneur and internationally recognized expert on relationships. Having brought on board an elite team of professionals from every corner of the world, together we aim to make our mark as one of the globe's paramount coaching organizations.

Our mission doesn't halt at fostering familial bonds. Much like families, organizations prosper when their members forge profound connections. Companies, at their crux, mirror Stone Age tribes—cohorts of individuals unified by a shared objective. As every tribal member was once anchored by a shared mission, so too must every individual in an organization resonate with its vision for authentic triumph.

This is the juncture where the Dietrich Institute galvanizes into action. We offer coaching and consultancy to individuals and organizations, ensuring that every stratum, from executive leadership to freshly inducted recruits, is deeply attuned to the company's ethos. Our mission is to build a tomorrow where personal evolution, heightened consciousness, and innate compassion stand tall as the bedrock of every institution, whether it's a nurturing household or a Fortune 500 company.

When I formally embarked on my coaching career, it was a natural step from the consulting and mentoring I was already involved in. Taking courses at Harvard and Wharton, among other institutions, I honed my skills in leadership and communication and qualified as a certified coach. Through the education programs I went through, I connected with experts and was referred to people who could help me grow.

One of the people I reached out to at this point was my friend Kiki, who I went to visit at the Curaçao Dolphin Therapy & Research Center in Curaçao.

The journey to Curaçao wasn't just a spontaneous vacation—it was a mission. After receiving an invitation from Kiki to witness the incredible work being done at the center, my wife and I were eager to visit. But beyond the allure of the beautiful island, I had an ulterior motive: to have a crucial conversation with Kiki.

We had been allies for nearly two decades, working together on coaching projects and in other fields, including philanthropy. Our bond transcended mere professional collaboration. I had witnessed her high level of expertise firsthand during our many ventures together.

When I arrived, the sun hung high in the azure Curaçao sky, casting a soft glow over the sandy beach. Families dotted the shores, their laughter punctuating the rhythmic lapping of waves. Amidst this paradise, Kiki and I sat in a beachside restaurant near the therapy center, at a table laden with light lunch offerings. The distant sounds of playing children and the delicate rustling of palm leaves swayed to the soft strains of background music.

Kiki was busy, deeply engrossed in a conference with almost fifty attendees. But she found time to meet me, reinforcing our strong bond of almost twenty years. Although my wife was there to support our cause, this luncheon was a personal tête-à-tête between two old friends.

Kiki was wearing her signature white dress, and her long blonde hair caught the sun's rays, creating a halo effect. Her sharp eyes, always reflective of her intelligence, studied me as I began to speak.

We began with pleasantries, then talked about her work at the therapy center and the experts she had recently been working with. From there, the conversation drifted to more personal topics, like the weight I had lost after my health scare and the emotional trauma from a recent betrayal by a close friend. She absorbed every word I uttered, sometimes with a nod and other times with an infectious chuckle, like when she teased me about *Fifty Shades of Grey* and my e-commerce endeavors. But it soon became clear that our true agenda that day was the Dietrich Institute.

"Think of it like the Mayo Clinic," I told her, drawing a parallel between their medical expertise and the coaching expertise I envisioned for the institute. "You go to Mayo knowing you'll get unparalleled care. I want the Dietrich Institute to be the equivalent in the realm of relationships, both individual relationships and those of organizations. My life, my experiences, have predestined me for this."

Kiki leaned forward, her gaze fixed intently on me. "You know, Tino," she began, her tone shifting to a blend of curiosity and caution, "the world of coaching is different. It's deep, it's vast. You've been successful with your e-commerce ventures, but this... this is different. Are you ready for it?"

"I don't expect to turn water into wine, Kiki. But I've lived, learned, and, most importantly, I've grown. I've come to realize that my true strength lies in understanding personal relationships. That's my calling. That's my true north."

For a moment, she held my gaze. Those sharp eyes of hers, always so revealing, seemed to penetrate my soul, assessing the authenticity and depth of my conviction.

"You have to be genuine, Tino," she finally said, her voice soft yet firm. "The journey you've been through, the trials, the betrayals… they've shaped you. Use them. Be real. Be you."

The intensity of our conversation was palpable. But then her demeanor softened, and she let out that wonderful laugh of hers. "I've always believed there was something more in store for you. I'm glad you've found it."

Feeling bolstered, I broached the topic that had weighed on me.

"Kiki," I began tentatively, "I'd like you to oversee both curriculum and content strategy at the Dietrich Institute. The role would be a dual one, as our Chief Coaching and Content Officer. Your expertise, your passion… I truly believe the institute would be incomplete without you at its helm."

She took a moment, her eyes searching mine. "Tino, I need to think about it. This is a big decision."

We stood up, and under the warmth of the Curaçao sun, our long, heartfelt hug symbolized more than just friendship. It hinted at a future partnership; it was a symbol of two forces uniting for a cause.

Kiki's words echoed in my ears long after our meeting, "This is something the world needs. And I know that you can do this, Tino."

A week after my return to Miami, I received a call. It was Kiki, her voice filled with conviction. "I'm in, Tino. Let's make this happen."

I knew that great things lay ahead.

I've realized, from having the conversation with so many people, how easy it is to confuse our purpose with mere goals. Do you know your true purpose? Can the elements of Ikigai help you articulate your true north? Coming to my purpose has given my life meaning. It has been a journey and a challenge I value with all my heart. Once the beacon of purpose lights the way forward, transformative change and genuine joy are the result.

7

THE CORNERSTONE OF CONNECTION

P ICTURE NEW YORK, a city bustling with people seeking connections, with cabs zipping past and twinkling lights from skyscrapers illuminating the night. In that teeming mass, one might ponder: What truly makes two souls click?

My friend Matthias, a sage in a business suit, once told me something that radically shifted my view on love and marriage.

An accomplished businessman with a legacy in the shipping industry, Matthias often imparted invaluable wisdom about life, love, leadership, and the lore of commerce. He had a family, a wife and two children, and resided in Cyprus. However, his business often took him between Hamburg, Cyprus, and other global destinations. Our bond deepened over time, and I had the privilege of accompanying him on numerous international journeys. The lessons I garnered from him are irreplaceable. At that juncture in my life, I was relatively inexperienced and somewhat naive. Serving as the deputy to a captain like Matthias was truly enlightening. He is sadly gone now, but still very present in my memories.

"Tino," he said to me once, "when you think of forever, think beyond the fire of passion. Envision the calm warmth of companionship, the shared laughter, and the silent understanding. Because the heart's true anchor isn't just romance; it's profound friendship."

In this chapter, there are myriad stories that highlight this, poignant truths from those who live on society's fringe—the candid confessions of a prostitute revealing the yearnings of her clients for not just physical but emotional solace, or a sex worker from the neon-lit streets of Vegas offering a moment of genuine human connection beyond mere physical intimacy. The startling revelations from these encounters unfurled before me a world where people often don masks, especially in matters of the heart. It's a dance of truths and half-truths, and it made me wonder: How often do we truly see and acknowledge the person beside us, stripped of pretense and façade?

In the tempest of our relationships, the beacon that guides us through the fog is connection. It's in the tiny gestures, the unsaid words, and the spaces in between where love truly resides. It's not just about seeing, but truly understanding. Connection requires clarity, and it isn't just a choice—it's a road map to a love that endures.

I've mentioned that at the Dietrich Institute the focus isn't only on romantic relationships, nor only on family, but on business relationships as well. The same values are at play in all. Being in a business relationship is like being in a family relationship, a friendship, a community. The same principles apply in all areas of life. A relationship is made up of individuals, and society is made up of a collection of relationships. How people function in their relationships is relevant to how they function in business, in society, in their community.

Diving deeper into the intricacies of human evolution, one uncovers a unique characteristic that sets us apart: our innate capability to bond and collaborate. It's not just our cognitive strength, but also our unparalleled ability to weave tales, form shared myths, and unite under collective beliefs that facilitate large-scale collaboration. This is a trait no other species possesses to the same extent. The beauty of human relationships transcends their mere existence. Each connection, whether familial, romantic, or business-related, has the power to harmonize disparate notes into a resonant melody. When individuals come together with shared intentions, the result is far greater than a simple arithmetic addition—it's a chorus of synchronized aspirations. Our true brilliance lies not just in our ability to connect, but also in our potential to elevate each connection, turning every bond into a timeless symphony.

Enduring friendship

In the vast spectrum of human connections, friendship holds a singular luminance. It's an alliance not birthed from obligation or tradition, but from vulnerable moments, shared laughter, and mutual respect. Friendships remind us that the most profound bonds can emerge from simple conversations, shared adventures, and the unspoken understanding that someone has your back. It's in these unscripted moments, where two souls converge and find harmony, that the true essence of the bond is uncovered.

Think about your friendships. I am lucky to have some strong, genuine friendships, but I've also experienced the opposite. There are some people who, if you need them and you call them for help, they will come, no matter what's happened. They will do everything in their power to be there for you, and you would do the same for them. Then there are others who you *think* are your friends. These are the people who, if you call them and it's raining, they're more likely to take away the umbrella they once gave you than help you through anything.

It's sad, but I've witnessed it firsthand. When you gain some success, when you start to make some money, people notice. They pick up on the façade of what they call "the good life." All of a sudden, everybody's there to dance to that music. They want to participate in your life, and that's all they want to do. When the music stops, they're gone. Very few stick around if the tune changes.

There's a line in a poem by Brian A. Chalker: "People come into your life for a reason, a season, or a lifetime." Life really is like that. Some of the hardest lessons you'll learn come from people you once trusted and considered your friends. Another saying, from my hometown, a harbor town, goes, "Ships are coming and ships are going." Similarly, people come and go. Some leave because of issues in their own life. Sometimes people change, and that takes them away. Perhaps they have a family, and so their priorities change. Success can change people, too. And so can betrayal. We talked earlier in this book about being burned by past relationships and the actions people take. That's not just a problem in romantic relationships.

TRUE FRIENDSHIPS VS. SUPERFICIAL CONNECTIONS

Throughout life, certain friendships shine brighter than others. In my journey, friends have come in and out, some leaving indelible marks, while others simply faded with time. Some acquaintances fluttered by like brief moments on a summer's day, while others nestled deep into my soul, becoming akin to family without sharing the same blood. But sometimes the melody of friendships can hit a sour note, especially when trust is betrayed. When someone close, close enough to be mistaken for family, opts for greed over our bond, the pain is sharper than any blade.

But here's my personal revelation: holding on to that resentment, that raw sense of betrayal, scalds my own heart. Science backs this up, linking unforgiveness to increased stress, potential heart disease, and a weakened immune system. So, every time I've faced such a wound, I've found solace in forgiveness—not to absolve someone of their misdeeds, but because I owe it to myself to find peace. Letting go is my act of self-love, ensuring I'm not weighed down by past heartaches. Because, ultimately, it's not just about forgiving them— it's also about granting myself the serenity to move on.

Yet again, clarity is key. The important thing is to recognize when people are true, when they can be relied upon. Such friends really can become family.

And there is one thing you can count on: good friends will ask you the hard questions.

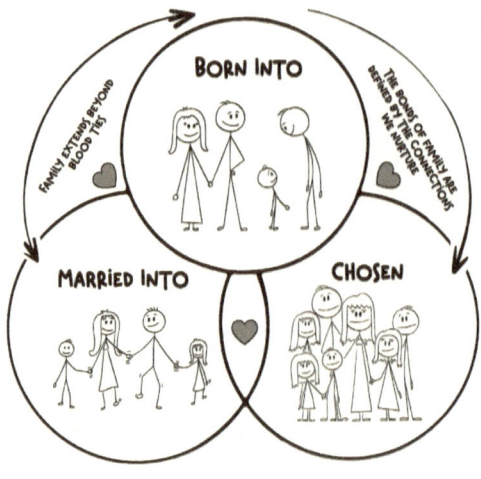

"Is she your best friend?"

I mentioned at the start of this chapter my good friend Matthias. When I was in my twenties, he was the elder brother I never had. It just goes to show how important your relationships are—they affect everything, from your own health and well-being to the health and well-being of your other relationships. If it weren't for my friend Matthias, I wouldn't be married to Silke.

In the fall of 1996, while I was visiting Matthias in Cyprus, we hopped in his car and drove to the top of a beautiful mountain. The view was spectacular—I could see the coastline of Turkey in the distance, across the deep blue expanse of the Mediterranean.

"I know you're getting more serious with your girl-friend," said Matthias, after we took a few moments to soak in the stunning scenery.

"I am," I admitted. "I'm in love with her."

He leaned in closer. "Falling in love is easy. Every-body falls in love. But that's not the same as wanting to make a lifelong commitment to another person."

Matthias had spent some time with my then-girl-friend and I, so I knew he was trying to tell me something.

"When you think you're serious about a woman, look at her again, but don't look at her like a lover. See her as the mother of your children. Imagine her with gray hair. Imagine her with lines on her face. Do you still love her?"

Matthias walked over to a boulder and sat down on it, looking out over the sea. I joined him and, for a while, we quietly enjoyed the setting sun.

"Marriage shouldn't feel like an obligation, some-thing that you're doing because you're the right age to do it," Matthias finally went on. "Young people, when they meet someone, someone beautiful and full of life, they want to marry right away. But those aren't the feelings you're looking for. Wait for someone you can't imagine living without. Not someone you always want to jump in bed with: someone you want to hold hands with, and feel their shoulder up against yours.

Ask yourself: Is she your best friend, and will she always be your best friend? That's when you know."

With this one conversation, Matthias gave me a whole new way to look at romantic relationships. I had thought I was very much in love, but after our talk, I quickly realized I was very much in lust. That girlfriend and I eventually wound up going our separate ways.

About a year and a half later, it was Matthias who played Cupid and brought me together with Silke. He invited us separately onto his boat for a weekend, his intentions as clear as a sunny day in Ibiza. He thought we'd be a great match, and I couldn't agree more. I'd fallen head over heels the first day I saw Silke in a café in Hamburg, certain she was the one, even though we were strangers. Weeks later, as I was too shy to speak, it was a friend who approached her for me. But it was that weekend orchestrated by Matthias that truly made things happen.

The first evening, I donned a bright pink sweater, thinking I was the epitome of fashion. When I stepped in front of my future wife, her stare made me feel as if I were wearing nothing at all.

"There's no way I'm going out with you wearing that," she declared.

That sweater, now presumed lost somewhere on a boat in Ibiza, still makes us laugh today. Thanks to Matthias's intervention, we celebrated our twenty-fifth anniversary in 2024, and this year (2025) will be our twenty-sixth anniversary.

Matthias's advice was invaluable to me, but I would never have been able to follow it if I didn't take the time to reflect deeply on my own expectations, hopes, and intentions. It was developing a strong relationship with myself that allowed me to discover what I wanted in and needed from a partner.

Wedding of Tino and Silke, September 18, 1999, Tegernsee Castle, Bavaria

Meeting the experts

Fast forward a whole bunch of years, and in 2008, my wife and I were standing in the bedroom while I packed for my next trip.

"You're doing *what?*" asked Silke.

"I need to go see a prostitute," I casually repeated, as I continued to pack clothes into my suitcase. "Actually, I'm going to probably see dozens of prostitutes."

I felt a laser-like burn on the back of my neck. I stopped packing and turned to meet my wife's glare.

"It's for work," I added, as if that explained the whole thing.

"For work," she repeated.

We were both fighting off the urge to smile. Her indignation was feigned, and we both knew it. This was another shared moment we'd remember fondly.

"Silke, should I continue to pack, or not?"

She was the first to crack a grin. "No, it's okay. I trust you."

At that time, I was rolling out an online dating service, and I traveled frequently for my work. All of that made me somewhat complicated as a spouse. Luckily, Silke has always accepted me for who I am, and I, in turn, accept her for who she is.

When I was finally ready to leave on my trip, I turned to Silke and kissed her. "I love you."

"I love you. Now go have fun with your prostitutes," she said, with a twinkle in her eye.

A few days after leaving home (as usual, with no intention of leaving my wife), I walked into one of Hamburg's most prestigious brothels. Whatever I'd been picturing (and whatever you're picturing now!), it felt more like the cigar lounge of a country club. I was looking for a woman in a skintight red dress, who I'd been told was one of the highest-paid sex workers in Germany. She had said she'd be at the bar on the first floor of the brothel, and had assured me I wouldn't be able to miss her.

And there indeed she was—no GPS needed here. From across the room, I could see her toying with her champagne flute. In addition to the dress, she was kitted out in knock-off Louboutin black pumps, extravagant makeup, and perfectly coiffed hair. We'll call her Claudia.

I sat down beside her. She glanced at me once, and then looked back at her glass. I followed her gaze and saw her intently twirling a little wooden spoon in her champagne. I'd never seen anyone do this before.

"What are you doing?"

"It's hydrophobic," she replied.

"Hydro … hydro-*what*?"

I thought hydrophobia was some kind of disease, or maybe a fear of something.

"Hydrophobic," she repeated. She continued to twirl the spoon.

"What's that mean?"

"It means it doesn't absorb the liquid, the spoon. Because it's wood. Like how you can lay a wooden spoon over a boiling pot of water, and it'll stop boiling over. The wood destabilizes the bubbles."

I had prepared for a lot of possibilities in this encounter, but I hadn't expected a chemistry lesson.

"So … you're trying to get rid of the bubbles?"

"Exactly."

"What's wrong with bubbles? I mean, isn't that kind of the whole idea with champagne?"

"The bubbles make you belch. And I'm working. Belching isn't very ladylike, is it?"

She had me there.

"Why not just drink wine? No bubbles in wine."

"I don't drink wine when I'm working. Wine is a bit proletarian, ordinary, gauche. Don't you think?"

I was learning a lot already.

I'd been clear up front that this encounter would be conversation-only. Our appointment had been set up by a third party, and I'd been assigned a different name to ensure anonymity. After a number of interviews, I discovered that these kinds of "dates"—ones that didn't involve any type of physical intimacy—were quite common in the profession. In fact, I learned that sex is only one of many components in the day-to-day routine of a sex worker. Conversation is the one thing that is common to all worker-client interactions; sex, not necessarily.

I will say that this experience gave me an appreciation for the art of interviewing. Many of my initial interviews hit dead ends and concluded early. Despite the safeguards in place to protect both of our identities, I found that it took time to develop a sense of trust with most of these women. In the beginning, I stuck to a rigid progression of questions, but I learned early on that this was a bad tactic. A more natural, back-and-forth dialogue produced much more interesting and insightful conversation.

In one of our interviews, Claudia told me, "The men that come here, they talk about work, their feelings, how they're underappreciated at home. They tell me stories about their friends, their families. Basically, they just unload everything that's on their minds. They think they're coming here for sex, but the real reason they're here is that they're looking for a way to share intimacy with someone, someone they can trust. For some reason, they don't have anybody else that they can do this with."

"Interesting," I said slowly. I scanned the room, thinking about how what she was saying would apply to each of the men here at the brothel.

Claudia gestured around the bar. "This is where we spend most of our time. This is our primary workplace." She pointed up toward the bedrooms. "They pay for an hour, but nobody lasts an hour up there."

She slid her little wooden spoon down the bar, and the bartender cleared it away.

As I wrapped up the interview, I thanked her for her time.

"Hey, no problem." She winked. "You sure this is all you need?"

Fourteen percent of married men have admitted to visiting a prostitute at least once.[11] That might seem like a relatively low number at first glance. But according to several of the women I interviewed, over ninety percent of the men who visit them are married. And many of these men visit the same prostitutes regularly, developing a relationship with them over time.

The consensus among the women that I spoke to was that sex is not the primary reason that their clients visit. Rather, they visit for conversation and intimacy; sex is secondary. What does that say about these men's marriages? Many of them may be having sex with their spouse, but it's intimacy that they're missing.

---

11 Welsh, J. "Prostitution Isn't as Common as You Might Think." *Business Insider* (March 2013).

At an adult expo in Las Vegas, I had the opportunity to meet one of the top-earning legal sex workers in the United States. The four-foot-eight employee of an establishment in Nevada, outside of Las Vegas, she has said that her most-requested service is what she calls "the girlfriend experience."

For the "girlfriend experience," she and her client take things to a level of intimacy beyond what most sex workers provide. They go out to eat together, or they might go to a concert. Between dates, they email and text. Sometimes they talk on the phone. They maintain a connection with each other and build a relationship. It goes well beyond a single, stand-alone session. But, of course, it's all on a professional basis.

For one reason or another, many men can't have, or don't want, a traditional one-on-one relationship, so they find someone like this woman to fill that void. This allows them to be in control of the duration of the intimacy and the form that it takes, without any maintenance or upkeep.

This sex-worker also works with couples who are looking for an experienced coach to help them jump-start their sex lives. She even offers lessons in advanced BDSM techniques, so for anyone who's ever wanted to learn how to properly tie your partner to the bedposts and flog them, she's your gal. And, of course, sex toys—no matter how much you think you know about sex toys, she still has plenty to teach you. She's truly a connoisseur of all things battery-powered and silicone.

But not everyone she works with is experienced enough to know what they enjoy. Many of her clients are adult virgins. Some of them have never been out on a date. With them, she starts with a gesture as simple as holding hands, and then, step by step, she takes them through the whole experience.

I seriously didn't expect to learn what I did speaking with these "sexperts." But this is a pattern that repeated for me throughout my quest to understand relationships. Whatever you think the reason behind something might be, be ready to learn that it isn't.

When it comes to the reason for all our misconceptions, there's a simple explanation: as the title of Seth Stephens-Davidowitz's book proclaims, *everybody lies*. "People lie, to friends, lovers, doctors, surveys—and themselves."[12] Especially when it comes to love, sex, and relationships. No wonder we're so fogged up.

In my conversations with sex workers in Germany, Austria, and the US, the common theme was that everyone craves intimacy—not just sex, but rather a feeling of connection. And it turns out that a whole lot of people aren't getting it. It seems that this experience, either of being single or of being in a relationship that's unfulfilling, is incredibly widespread. So, what does that say about our abilities to form and maintain meaningful relationships? What are the pitfalls that people encounter as they try to navigate their romantic and sexual relationships?

---

12 Stephens-Davidowitz, S. (2017). *Everybody Lies: What the Internet Can Tell Us About Who We Really Are*. Bloomsbury.

And how can those problems be avoided or solved in healthy, long-lasting ways?

These are some of the questions I've set out to explore with the Dietrich Institute.

Would it kill you to pay me a compliment?

Taking my role seriously when I was working in the industry, I registered accounts on various online dating platforms, including ours—not for personal intentions, but for professional insight. My happily married status was transparent to all my colleagues, my wife was informed, and I conversed only with women in the US while in Switzerland, ensuring there were no misconceptions about a possible physical relationship. The goal was purely to understand users' needs and service functionality. No one was misled, though deep conversations did occur.

One in particular sticks out for me. I will never forget the lovely woman whose picture on the site was a selfie taken in her car. In the back seat, you could see two kids' car seats in the back of the vehicle.

When we messaged, she told me about the misery she was living. Married with kids, her husband's family was very present in their lives, while her husband himself was not. There was little lovemaking, few gestures of intimacy. His family was very dominant; she was made to feel the need to serve them. She received no kind words, no acknowledgement. In fact, since being a kid, she'd had little affection bestowed on her.

Her friend had told her about our site, and that's how she'd ended up on there. But she didn't know what she was looking for, and there was no enjoyment in it for her. As we chatted, it became clear how underappreciated she felt, how alone.

I paid her a simple compliment, saying it was a pity. I told her, "If I woke up to a smile like yours, I would feel lucky."

The next day I had a message from her, telling me she was deregistering. She said, "Thank you for yesterday's chat. You made my day. My month. My year."

And that was it—she was gone. She had gotten what she needed, and it wasn't sex; it wasn't an affair. She was tired of trying to please all the time with no acknowledgement. A simple compliment had lit her up.

In the labyrinth of love and commitment, the allure of the forbidden often presents itself, enticing many to stray from their path. However, my epiphany was this: the act of straying is not the genesis of relationship woes, but rather an outcome of something deeper, more fundamental.

The shimmering allure of an extramarital affair is often not the root of the decay, but merely a manifestation. The apple of temptation, juicy and enticing, is falling not because the sky willed it so, but because the tree from which it hung was already ailing.

No one deeply in love and content in their commitment wakes up with the deliberate thought of betraying that sacred bond. Yet, affairs happen. They are often the desperate cries of souls yearning for something missing, something unspoken, or something neglected in the relationship. Every affair has a backstory, as unique and varied as the whorls of a fingerprint or the venation of a leaf.

Throughout my journey in the tangled world of relationships, I've borne witness to the heart-wrenching tales behind such affairs. Every couple, every story, has presented nuances that were deeply personal and yet strikingly universal. And while one could pen tomes on this complex tapestry of love, betrayal, and redemption, one sentiment stands clear—it's not about the forbidden fruit, it's about nurturing the tree.

When was the last time you told your significant other that you truly appreciate what they do for you? And when was the last time you were acknowledged like that—told by someone, truly, honestly, what you mean to them?

I'd love to sit on the set of *Good Morning America* and pose that very question. While a public response isn't necessary, deep inside, each individual knows their truth better than anyone else. Before you ponder the fallen apple, perhaps it's time to ask yourself: Is there something amiss with the tree? Go take care of the roots before the next apple falls.

Clear things up

So, what's the solution to life, the universe, and everything? What's the secret to relationships? (There's always a solution, and actually it's not some big, mysterious secret.)

As an old friend of my mom's always used to say, "You have to clear things up."

Her name was Tini, and she could have walked straight out of a Hollywood movie. But I'm not talking about sex appeal—she just lit up the room. Wherever she went, she was the life of the party, the center of attention. She told the funniest stories and had the most wonderful laugh. But her greatest qualities were her presence and her intelligence—her good sense. She was entirely present when she was with you, conscious in a way few people are. And she was smart about life. She had clarity. Her consciousness came from her clarity, and her clarity came from her consciousness—the two are closely intertwined.

Whenever there was something going on with my mom, she would come around. She'd cut straight through the mess to the heart of the issue. She would ask the right questions. And then, the path forward out of the fog would become obvious. She helped light the way.

Remember, though, that while we may be lucky enough to have guides like Tini, *you* are in charge of your own clarity. If you want to move forward, you need to ask yourself the right questions. Wipe those fogged-up glasses clean.

You have to clear things up.

Do you have clarity around your relationships? Do you feel like something is missing? The beacon of connection sheds light on the ties that bind us to other people, not just our chosen partners but also our family, our friends, our colleagues, our neighbors, and our community.

8

STOPPING THE CLOCK—THE FUTURE OF RELATIONSHIPS

A T THE TIME of writing, if you entered "AI tells" into Google, the top search result was: "AI tells man to leave wife." A *New York Times* technology columnist had recently described his unease speaking with "Sydney" the chatbot, who declared that it was in love with him, in an article warning about the emergent abilities of AI and what they might mean for humanity.[13]

---

13 Roose, K. "A Conversation with Bing's Chatbot Left Me Deeply Unsettled." *The New York Times*, February 2023. Accessed online 15 April 2023. https://www.nytimes.com/2023/02/16/technology/bing-chatbot-microsoft-chatgpt.html

At the same time, there was backlash from human users when the chatbot Replika was modified to cease sexting. The "AI companion" bot's premium service involved exchange of lewd images as well as the ability to sext. The loss of this was described as traumatic, raising worries that the ensuing struggles faced by deprived users would even prompt some to attempt suicide.[14]

This all seems pretty wild, but just look at how things have changed over the decades, even before AI. In 2011, one UK study named Facebook as a major contributor to a third of divorce petitions[15] (ever looked up your high-school sweetheart on social media and been tempted to reconnect?). And just look at people's porn consumption. It used to be that people accessed it (by accident, of course) on the X-rated channel they found in a hotel room. Nowadays, it's on people's phones twenty-four-seven. It's had a massive effect on society. It's become a determining factor in how kids learn about intimacy (which is a whole other conversation). It's a normal part of life—people watch it *all the time*.

If you're in any doubt, let's look at the data.

---

14 Al-Sibai, N. "Users Furious as AI Girlfriend App Suddenly Shuts Down Sexual Conversations." *The Byte*, February 2023. Accessed online 15 April 2023. https://futurism.com/the-byte/replika-users-furious

15 Wilkinson & Finkbeiner, "Divorce Statistics: Over 115 studies, facts and rates for 2022." wf-lawyers.com. Accessed online 4 August 2023. https://www.wf-lawyers.com/divorce-statistics-and-facts/

Four of the top twenty most-visited websites in the United States are pornography-related. The top two porn websites alone net an average of 1.3 *billion* visits from US users per month.[16] (For context, the total adult population of the US is about 260 million.) That's a lot of skin.

And yet, despite the fact that porn websites outrank the likes of Netflix and Zoom, there's still a heavy stigma attached to this popular pastime. If you ask most people if they've visited adult websites, you'll likely get a lot of wide-eyed *"who, me?"* looks. Some might say, "Once in a while, but just by accident."

Yep, sure. Accidents. In fact, 1.3 billion of 'em.

Lying about our porn habits is a time-honored tradition, which has made it difficult for scientists to get an accurate estimate of just how many people consume porn and in what forms. But these days, researchers don't need to rely on self-reporting: they've got our Google data, and that's a whole lot more honest than most of us would ever be. In surveys, roughly twenty-five percent of men and eight percent of women are willing to admit that they watch porn. And yet, according to Seth Stephens-Davidowitz, data scientist and author of *Everybody*

---

16 Khalili, Joel. "These Are the Most Popular Websites Right Now—And They Might Just Surprise You." TechRadar, July 13, 2021. https://www.techradar.com/news/porn-sites-attract-more-visitors-than-netflix-and-amazon-youll-never-guess-how-many.

Lies, "there have historically been more searches for porn than for weather."[17]

What does this mean for the future of relationships—especially given the advent of AI, which is only going to get more and more sophisticated and easier and easier to access? Well, we're faced with the frozen pizza problem.

The frozen pizza problem

Back in our species' prehistory, our ancestors had to hunt the food they needed to sustain themselves; you can picture it in your head now, a group of cavemen setting out to hunt a woolly mammoth. But the mammoths were surprisingly fast, hunting was exhausting, and so you had to forage to sustain yourself along the way. You found some berries, and they kept you going. They were convenient, the least energy-consuming option, the path of least resistance.

Fast forward to today, and those berries are now frozen pizza. Boom. It's so easy. You don't want to cook all the time, and here's a full meal ready to go. The issue is when you start to think, *You know what? Hey, I don't want to run after the mammoth anymore.* And you start eating frozen pizza every day, which everyone would agree is not the best for your health. It's convenience food.

---

17 Khazan, Olga. "Our Searches, Ourselves." *The Atlantic.* Atlantic Media Company, June 9, 2017. https://www.theatlantic.com/health/archive/2017/06/our-searches-our-selves/529740/.

And that's exactly what AI is going to become. It takes effort to maintain a relationship; it can be exhausting sometimes, communicating and navigating conflict with another human being. As we've discussed, for many people it's often more convenient to go and see a prostitute to experience intimacy than it is to battle through issues with a partner. It's easier to talk to a stranger (one who'll encourage you to buy a second bottle of champagne). They won't argue with you or try and change your point of view. A one-night stand with no strings attached is more convenient than figuring out how to coexist with someone and care for them day in and day out.

AI takes that kind of freedom even further. Here, there truly is no obligation—but also no nutrition. Like porn, like alcohol, it becomes a drug that takes the edge off. And the more society accepts it—the more that AI companions become the norm—the less of a question it will be as to whether it's actually good for you. Sure, there are documentaries about what our unhealthy habits are doing to us, health warnings on the backs of cigarette packets, and nutritional information displayed at our fast-food chains these days—but is there a big sign above your local burger joint that reads, "Hey, if this is your hundredth cheeseburger this week, maybe consider cooking up some unprocessed food?"

It would be easy for AI to fill the intimacy hole for a lot of people. VR porn, prostitution robots—the whole nine yards, just like an episode of *Black Mirror*.

It all exists already—the complete virtual experience of intimacy, engaging all the senses, capable of paying you the compliments that light you up, holding a conversation, speaking like it cares, doing all the things that make you feel good. But what will be missing is that soul connection. Community.

From the very beginnings of our history, how did we survive? By banding together. Gathering around the fire. Helping each other hunt and forage. Supporting and protecting each other. Raising the children as a village. That is what relationships are.

I'm reminded here of *Sapiens* by Yuval Noah Harari, a book that peels back the layers of the Homo sapiens story. As we navigate the path ahead, it's hard not to wonder: What if AI becomes the composer of our connections, forging our bonds?

Picture it—holograms and AI chatbots, echoes of *Blade Runner 2049*, poised to play roles in our intimate lives. But as this saga unfolds, the concern lingers: Might AI-driven relationships steer us away from the very essence that propelled our evolution? You see, *Sapiens* tells us that it's our ability to forge complex relationships that sets us apart from other creatures.

Harari reveals that our cooperative nature propelled us to build civilizations, to thrive as a species. Our stories bound us, connected us, and fueled our collective ascent. But what if those narratives, those connections, are penned by AI instead? Are we poised at the edge of a new chapter, where AI, not our innate social bonds, shapes our course?

The issue is: Can AI ever replicate the spontaneity, the intimacy, the unpredictability that comes with human connection? Can AI be more than a surrogate, or will it always just mimic the dance while being devoid of the music?

There are warning signs ahead. But perhaps the best road to take is not to abandon the tools that AI offers, but to make sure we wield them as extensions of our humanity, not replacements.

So, as we write this next chapter together, let's remember that while AI might sketch the backdrop, the protagonists must always be us. The continued tale of Homo sapiens hinges on our capacity to form connections beyond mere transaction. As we step into the future hand in hand with AI, let's ensure that the stories we pen remain authentically human—with threads of vulnerability, laughter, and love that AI can't replicate, no matter how advanced it becomes.

We have to beware of the normalization of artificial experience. We need to have faith in humanity—in each other. And we have to be willing to do the work. To engage clarity, consciousness, and compassion. To not be robbed of our independent thinking. We need to remember our values, and put faith in the importance of our relationships.

There's a choice when it comes to the future. It doesn't have to be bleak. It will take a countermovement. We don't want to exist on frozen pizza alone.

Sure, every so often, let's enjoy it. I'm not opposed to exploring the benefits of AI, but we need to remember ourselves. We want warmth and security. A home. We want to love and be loved. Just because it's difficult doesn't mean it can't be done.

On that note, let's bring the conversation back to today.

The reality of the American Dream

Did you know that almost fifty percent of marriages in the US today end in divorce or separation? Fifty percent. Almost half. To break that down, that's forty-one percent of first marriages, sixty percent of second marriages, and seventy-three percent of third marriages.[18] Shockingly, the US has the sixth-highest divorce rate in the world; it's beaten only by the likes of Russia, Belarus, and Gibraltar. What is going on? We're looking at a couple getting divorced every forty-two seconds. Eighty-six divorces per hour. Over two thousand a week. Nearly 750,000 divorces a year. There are nearly three divorces in the time it takes a couple to recite their wedding vows.[19]

Many might be quick to point a finger at infidelity as the prime reason for divorce. But here's the thing: citing cheating as the primary cause is, in many ways,

---

18 Wilkinson & Finkbeiner. *Op cit.*

19 *Ibid.*

misleading. The act of cheating isn't the root of the problem; it's often a painful symptom of a deeper, unresolved issue. Think about it—if a person is genuinely content and fulfilled in their marriage, the thought of being unfaithful doesn't enter their mind. The real culprits often precede the act of infidelity itself. If these core issues are not addressed and we choose to remarry, we can unknowingly carry that same baggage into our new relationship. This baggage, unchecked, could be the very reason why second marriages frequently see a higher divorce rate, with about two-thirds ending in separation.

So, if it isn't just about infidelity, then what is it? A national survey sheds some light on this. Infidelity ranked third in the list of common reasons for divorce. The top two reasons? Arguing incessantly took the second spot, but the primary reason was a lack of commitment. And following closely behind infidelity were other reasons, such as marrying too young and stepping into marriage with unrealistic expectations. This all goes to show that it's essential to dig deeper and understand the foundational cracks before diagnosing the problem.

When you look at these statistics, it's devastating. And that's just the bottom level. Let's take a step back. Think about the American Dream. Equality, justice, democracy. Why do people come to the States? They want to make it here. They want to provide for their families. Some immigrants reach the country with the very last drop of their energy. They come to empower their children to have a better life.

As Sarah Churchill writes for *The Catalyst*, "No less an authority than the *Oxford English Dictionary* defines the American Dream as 'the ideal that every citizen of the United States should have an equal opportunity to achieve success and prosperity through hard work, determination, and initiative.'"[20] Yet what's the reality? Almost half of America's kids growing up as children of divorce.

Children of divorce grow up more likely to get divorced themselves. It's a vicious cycle. And I want to cut off the air to this toxic greenhouse. I want to stop this clock ticking; that "ding" every forty-two seconds signifying yet another divorce. It doesn't have to be this way. Let's slow it down, year on year. Remember my motto—one less asshole? Let's do the same thing with divorce.

My parents weren't married; they split up before I was born. My father then married, divorced, and remarried. This all puts me on the scale, given the statistics, with a much lower chance of being in a healthy relationship. And in all honesty, I'm not saying it's my contributions that have led to my marriage being a successful one. The reason my relationship is where it is today is togetherness. My wife and I have worked hard and weathered a lot of storms: bad health, miscarriages, economic crises, a global pandemic (which, by the way, has likely increased divorce rates even further)... you name it. You might say we're still together against the odds.

---

20 Churchill, S. "A Brief History of the American Dream." *The Catalyst*, 2021. Accessed online 4 August 2023. https://www.bushcenter.org/catalyst/state-of-the-american-dream/churchwell-history-of-the-american-dream

As well as seeing the struggles growing up with a single mom, and everything she had to go through, I also saw how my grandmother was left. Her husband was taken away by a "greater cause," but the end result was she was left with four boys to raise on her own. I want fewer broken families. I want more kids growing up with a father.

When it comes to my marriage, the key is balance. A lot of things have been thrown at us to try to push us off-balance, but we've been able to hold it together. The anchor in the storms that have kept our ship in place are our shared values, beliefs, and traditions. Our commitment to living with clarity, consciousness, and nobility. We are co-pilots, both of us in the cockpit at the controls of the plane. When we hit turbulence, we hit it together. We have in each other a safe haven, a lifesaver.

Of course, we've wandered off track from time to time. No one and nothing is perfect. But the important thing is we always come back together. It's not about the conflicts that come up or the fights we have; it's how we manage them.

Everything is connected. Everyone is connected. We each need to cultivate a sense of interconnectedness and oneness with the world around us. To recognize that we are part of a larger whole and act with empathy, compassion, and unity. Each individual can't just go around taking care of their own shit; we have shared shit to take care of.

I don't just want to slow this clock down, getting that forty-two seconds up to over a minute; I want to set an alarm. It's time for a wake-up call. There's no time to waste. I want to touch millions of couples, and help them gain the clarity they need to see, hear, and communicate in a compassionate way. Together, we can help heal the damage being done to society. We can help heal the damage being done to our children.

The issues I became familiar with in the online dating industry and the realizations the data has fueled for me have put me in a place where I can try and tackle this divorce pandemic.

Bringing back family values

Everyone deserves a loving home. And it's possible.

Susanne, my first love at sixteen, has remained a cherished friend over the years. Our bond is so deep that she's now the godmother to my eldest son, Corbinian. Our families have intertwined, with her husband and children being as close to my wife and kids as relatives.

Some people find this crazy in itself: that I could be such close friends with an ex-girlfriend, that my wife could possibly be friends with her. What does that say about us and our perception of intimate relationships?

Suffice to say, we're like family. And when I think of genuine, loving relationships—a successful marriage—I think of Susanne's parents, Ulle and Fred, who were like second parents to me. Fred became very ill a couple of years ago, and to his very last day on this earth, Ulle was there for him. They were married to each other the majority of their lives, and they took that commitment seriously. At the end of Fred's life, it became very tough, but Ulle took care of her husband. They raised wonderful children and demonstrated to them all the elements of a loving relationship. They proved that a loving, lasting relationship is possible, guided by family values. That, to me, is love.

Family values are the bedrock that traditionally held relationships together, a lighthouse guiding us through the stormy seas of life. But in recent years, many have thrown these tried-and-true principles overboard, replacing them with deceptive beliefs that only serve to muddy the waters. Today's society often values immediate gratification over long-term commitment (frozen pizza, anyone?), superficial charm over deep connection, and personal gain over shared growth. The result? A staggering increase in failed relationships.

About sixty percent of couples who marry between the ages of twenty and twenty-five end up divorcing. Why? Many of these young lovebirds tie the knot with their high-school sweetheart, only to realize the ensuing marriage doesn't align with their expectations. Many aren't even sure what those expectations were in the first place.

But let's dive deeper into that intoxicating phenomenon known as falling in love. Ever felt like you were losing your mind when falling head over heels for someone? Well, science has an explanation for that. When you fall in love, the brain releases a cocktail of chemicals, including dopamine and oxytocin, that leads to feelings of euphoria and attachment. But here's the kicker: the prefrontal cortex, the part of the brain responsible for rational decision-making, tends to take a little vacation during this phase. This explains why new lovers often overlook red flags and make impulsive decisions. It's not just poetic rhetoric; studies have shown that romantic love leads to decreased activity in areas of the brain associated with judgment and decision-making.

The fallout from these "brain vacations" and the abandonment of time-honored family values is more than individual heartbreak. It's contributing to a societal shift in which the very foundations of family and commitment are cracking under the weight of misaligned expectations and impulsive decisions. But there's hope. My purpose, my mission, extends beyond helping couples and families navigate these murky waters. It's about helping individuals, especially the young, to find their way and reconnect with those values that withstand the test of time. It's about building a future where relationships are nurtured with wisdom, clarity, and compassion, where we recognize that falling in love doesn't have to mean falling into confusion.

I can't help but think of my in-laws as I write these words. Their home is nestled not far from my hometown of Hamburg, which has allowed us frequent visits. My father-in-law, Dr. Hans-Juergen Werbatus, stands as an embodiment of unwavering commitment and profound love. My mother-in-law, Birgit Werbatus, endured a prolonged illness, and her final years were particularly tough. Throughout this time, Hans-Juergen was her rock, her steadfast companion. His dedication never wavered, nor did he ever voice any complaint, despite the profound weight of their shared circumstances. Every action, every gesture, echoed the promise of being there "in good times and in bad."

The poignancy of their story took a deeper turn during the Covid pandemic. Tragically, Birgit passed away in the midst of it, and the situation was made even more heart-breaking as my wife couldn't even be there to bid her mother a final farewell, due to restrictions.

Observing Hans-Juergen's unwavering dedication was humbling. His love for Birgit, his devotion to her in the face of adversity, exemplified the depth of true commitment. Their relationship, especially in its final chapter, illuminated the essence of genuine love and family values, even in the face of life's cruelest challenges.

Their story serves as a luminous example in our lives. Amidst the shadows and challenges we face, the love and devotion exhibited by Hans-Juergen is a light in the darkness, reminding us of the power of unwavering commitment and the beauty of enduring love.

Family values are everything. It is possible to foster them, nurture them, pass them on through generations. It is possible to grow together, conquer adversity together, and come out stronger, individually and collectively.

Together, let's envision a world where that is the norm. Where we're no longer talking about fifty percent divorce rates, but about enduring values, meaningful purpose, and genuine fulfillment. A world where we achieve clarity, not just in our marriages, but in all our relationships. In every aspect of our lives.

Let's build this future together.

Sharing golf with my son Caspar at Pebble Beach's 7th hole.
Moments of connection are what we're fighting to preserve.

CONCLUSION
A CALL TO ACTION

HAPPINESS IS not something we need to search for. It's something we're instinctively born with. Can you imagine telling an infant to be happy? Of course not—they're simply happy. As author Mo Gawdat says, "The default state is happiness."[21]

My friend Kiki holds to the belief that "Happiness is a choice." I would add to this, "And so is worry."

Worry is also a choice. As a child, happiness may be non-negotiable, but as an adult, life's many complications get in the way of this inherent joy. The key to returning to it is to live a simple, intentional life rather than a needlessly complex one.

As an individual, if you're not happy, then you can't share love and affection with another person.

---

21 Gawdet, M. (2019). *Solve for Happy: Engineer your path to joy.* Pan Macmillan.

Only the cup that overflows can share. It really is as easy, and as difficult, as that.

Think of a moment in your relationship when you felt utter joy. Maybe it was when you gave the dog a bath and she shook water all over the two of you, and neither of you could stop laughing. Maybe it was the weekend you and your partner spent together in the bedroom. Maybe it was just chatting in the morning over coffee. Whatever it was, ask yourself—how can you give yourselves more of that joy?

It's our thought process that creates our view of the world. To a certain degree, stress and trauma are unavoidable. But it's the way we deal with these things on a daily basis that determines our happiness and joy. There's something reassuring in that: it means that both happiness and love are essentially a choice. There is *always* something you can do, even when it feels like situations are out of your control.

Think of the film *Life is Beautiful*, in which a father convinces his son that the concentration camp where they've been imprisoned is actually just part of an elaborate game, where the winner receives a tank. For many, finding humor and levity in a place like that seems unthinkable. But it's simply a matter of the mind. Once the decision to seek joy has been made, no one can take it away.

Remember, you are in control of your own clarity.

TRUE CLARITY

Imagine you have a shimmering gold coin in your palm. Its weight feels genuine, and the gleam is unmistakably that of pure gold. You're proud of this treasure, and you decide to share its brilliance with someone else. As you open your hand to reveal the coin, they look at it and say, "That's just a worthless piece of metal."

Now, you're faced with a choice. You could spend your energy trying to convince them, showing every marking and proving its authenticity. But deep down, you know the truth of what you hold. Their opinion, while loud, cannot change the gold's inherent value. The clarity you have about the gold's authenticity is unwavering.

However, this also serves as a lesson. It reminds you to periodically examine the treasures of your beliefs and values. To hold them up against the light of truth, to ensure they are genuine and not merely what you've been told or want to believe. Because it's only when you have unwavering clarity about yourself and your convictions that you can stand firm in the face of doubt or opposition.

Fostering happiness in your relationships and in your life starts with making a choice. It won't happen overnight. But if you keep at it, I promise, it will happen. Choosing joy is a journey of endless growth. We're never complete. That's what's so amazing about being alive.

A new starting point

At a certain stage, we reach a new starting point. A point where we have the potential to change. And it's an epiphany.

I want you, from now on, for the rest of your life, to always remember when you run into a fight, when you don't know where to go, when you contemplate a career change, a new job, an offer, a project, it doesn't matter what—to ask yourself: "Do I have clarity?"

We've been walking around wearing fogged-up glasses, and it's time to wipe them clear. We need clarity in our life. We need to go back to the beginning, when we were kids, and get back that clarity.

When we're young, we enjoy what we enjoy— things that, when we're older, we don't let ourselves do. As kids, we find it easy to learn. As adults, less so.

As adults, our values have been shaped, determining what we do. The rules that we've been taught by our environment, by our parents and others, dictate how we see our life. That's how we grow up. The values, the beliefs, the rules, the environment—it all adds up and makes the way that you yourself would want to go less and less defined.

For some, like me, it takes a near-death experience to shake you up in such a way that you can suddenly see clearly again. But I think it doesn't have to take that. The whole point of the Dietrich Institute and our mission is to help people and organizations get to clarity without facing that kind of crisis.

When I was in the ICU, I said to myself, "Something is missing. I don't feel complete. I can't leave Earth." And so, thankfully as it turns out, I didn't.

I said, "I don't want to leave Earth this way. I don't want to leave my life, because I feel incomplete. I feel that I have not fulfilled my purpose." And at the same time, I was asking myself, "Okay, I haven't served my purpose. So, what *is* my purpose?"

It's time to look at things in a different way. We usually don't, because we always think in the back of our mind, "Oh, I have more than a year to live, surely." But just ask yourself: "Is this it? Is this the life I've always envisioned for myself? Is this the life I want to live? Are the things that are happening to me the things that I want to happen to me?"

If something is lacking, it's time to ask yourself: "What is it that's missing?"

For me, it was clearly not a third car. It was clearly not another watch. It was clearly not another holiday somewhere fancy. It was something actually meaningful. My purpose.

I dug deep, and now I'm living up to my potential. My purpose is to empower people to elevate their state of mind, to allow them to get to the same realization that I got to.

It all comes back to those words I heard Tini speak as a boy: "You have to clear things up."

It's time we all unfog our lives.

AFTERWORD
WTF (WHISPERS
TO FAMILY)

SHORTLY AFTER COMPLETING *UNfogged*, I had an encounter that crystallized all the themes and threads I'd been exploring, bringing into sharp focus the fundamental question at the heart of the project—the "why." After returning from one of my frequent business trips, I found myself in the warmth of our cozy kitchen during a rare family gathering. My eldest son, Corbinian—who had recently completed his bachelor's degree with honors from Bentley University and moved to Minneapolis for a position at an investment banking firm—had come home for a long weekend visit.

As we began catching up, our conversation quickly deepened. His youthful curiosity mirrored my own constant quest for answers as he questioned the path I'd chosen.

"But why?" he asked, his brow furrowing slightly. "Wasn't there anything else you could've done after recovering? Like becoming the CEO of another company, or joining an established one in a different leadership role?"

The question was a natural one. I explained that while I had indeed been a Founder and CEO several times, with experience that could have led to another top corporate role, my entrepreneurial spirit had always guided me toward building something new. During my recovery, I'd had time to reflect deeply on my life choices. I realized that true happiness isn't solely about wealth or traditional success—it's about aligning our actions with our passions, our values, and a greater purpose. It's about living authentically and making a positive impact on others' lives.

Looking thoughtful, Corbinian observed that my career might seem scattered to some, with ventures across various industries. Like an explorer charting unknown territory, my path had indeed taken me to many different shores. But what appeared scattered was actually part of a larger journey of self-discovery. I explained how the past twenty years had helped me gain a deeper understanding of myself and the world, leading me to where my passions, skills, and values could truly converge. During that process, I learned that my purpose—my 'why'—was to empower individuals and families to lead fulfilling lives.

"You see," I explained to Corbinian, "our world is filled with incorrect beliefs and values. I call them 'crules'—cruel rules that stop us from growing and achieving our dreams. They're akin to fear, which stands for 'false (or future) events appearing real.'"

CRULES

The crux of CRULES: Society's norms and expectations that often masquerade as guidance, but can lead us astray, fogging up our path to purpose, true happiness, the right choices, and our authentic selves.

As we talked, the aroma of home cooking filled the air. Silke, Caspar, and Lissy joined us at the table, fresh from preparing dinner. True to her nature of encouraging open family discussion, Silke asked about our conversation. After Corbinian's brief overview, she urged me to elaborate further.

I reminded them of Yuval Noah Harari's fascinating perspective on humanity—a concept I'd often shared with my family through his books. Harari explores humans' unique ability to connect their minds, not just through physical evolution, but through our capacity to collaborate, share knowledge, and work together on a grand scale. This harmony of minds leading to great achievements had become the cornerstone of my own journey to help people live harmoniously together.

Our values, beliefs, and the rules governing our interactions shape our collective identity and guide our actions toward a common purpose. Both history and scientific research remind us that our ability to cooperate and align on shared principles has been a driving force in our species' journey through time.

But even though we share so many beliefs and principles with others, we can't always connect through them. Those "crules"—the societal norms that create a fog obscuring our vision—get in the way. Take the belief that success can solely be measured by material wealth. Many chase money thinking it will bring happiness, only to find themselves unfulfilled and disconnected from their true passions and purpose.

To illustrate this point, I shared a parable that had profoundly impacted my perspective, one that connects directly to the Japanese concept of Ikigai central to my mission. Three bricklayers were asked what they were doing. The first replied, "I'm laying bricks to feed my family." The second answered, "I'm building a wall." The third, eyes cast to the sky, said, "I'm building a great cathedral to the Almighty."

The story perfectly illustrates how perspective and approach shape our destiny. Finding your Ikigai means discovering that deeper sense of purpose beyond mundane tasks, aligning your actions with your passion, values, and what the world truly needs.

Caspar, warming to the discussion, connected this to Steve Jobs's story about efficiency in movement. Jobs had referenced a study comparing different animals' movements over distance. While the condor topped the list and humans ranked only a third of the way down, a human on a bicycle could surpass even the condor. Our capacity as tool builders allows us to overcome natural limitations—just as computers became another tool amplifying our abilities, a bicycle for the mind. The transformation this brought to global communication exemplifies what we can achieve when connecting our minds and working together.

This concept of tools helped me elaborate on my mission. Our minds are our most formidable tools, but realizing their potential requires the right environment. Security, love, and supportive relationships create the foundation for unlocking our true potential.

Corbinian's own experience in investment banking had already shown him how crucial building strong relationships is, not just personally but professionally. Creating harmonious environments and nurturing positive relationships becomes a game-changer for companies and individuals alike.

Caspar added his perspective from sports, particularly golf, noting how the psychology behind working together and building relationships with coaches and competitors makes a crucial difference in performance.

The conversation turned to the concerning statistics about divorce rates and children growing up without fathers in the US. This touches the heart of my mission. I'm not content to merely witness these issues—I want to slow down the rate of divorce and transform houses into homes filled with love, support, respect, and compassion. Having grown up without a father present, while being raised by a hardworking single mother who did an incredible job, I understand firsthand what's at stake. While I have immense respect for single parents, it's not fair to them or to the children to accept this as inevitable.

My mission is to help couples build stronger, lasting relationships and give families the tools and knowledge to navigate life's challenges together rather than apart. Though my career path might look scattered, everything has been tied together by this single purpose: helping people recognize that their choices are at the heart of their challenges.

Silke reinforced this point, noting how we've always tried to raise our children with the understanding that their choices matter and that finding purpose is a journey worth pursuing. It's about discovering one's Ikigai, that harmonious blend of passions, talents, societal needs, and opportunities.

Lissy, who had been listening quietly, reminded us of Khalil Gibran's poem "On Children," which speaks to how children aren't really "ours" but are born through us and belong to the future. It perfectly captured our responsibility to nurture, guide, and create supportive environments where families can thrive and build better futures.

Our family, like any other, has faced its share of discord and disagreement. But moments like these remind us of our extraordinary bond. Perfection itself is another "crule" that can ensnare us—it's acknowledging our imperfections that truly brings us closer together.

As we finished our meal, Corbinian raised his glass. "To family, to purpose, and to the future." We clinked glasses, our connection fortified, ready to face life's challenges together, armed with purpose, love, and the wisdom of our shared journey.

ACKNOWLEDGMENTS

WRITING A BOOK is a journey on its own; at least it was for me. I began shaping the ideas for this book long before the world was gripped by the pandemic. Then, when Covid-19 struck, it wasn't just a health crisis but a profound turning point in my life. It altered not only my plans to write a book but also the trajectory of my existence. It transformed the idea of a book into a transformative voyage, one that I am thrilled to share with you today.

As I journeyed back in time, reflecting on the moments and situations that fill these chapters, I was flooded with memories, both joyful and challenging. It reminded me how fortunate I am to have crossed paths with countless extraordinary individuals, each of whom has contributed to the tapestry of my life. They have shaped my experiences, nurtured my growth, and provided the valuable lessons that have fueled my writing.

This book wouldn't have come to fruition without the wisdom, experiences, stories, and passion of these incredible people. I have been humbled by the privilege of collaborating with them, and I am immensely grateful for their indelible mark on my life's journey. These relationships have breathed life into my existence, molding me into the person I am today.

I extend my heartfelt gratitude to everyone who has made this book a reality. Some of you actively contributed to piecing it together, while others have stood steadfastly by my side, leaving an indelible mark on my heart and memories. To those who left us all too soon, you continue to live in my memories and in the stories I share. I am eternally grateful for the time we had together.

I want to acknowledge and express my deepest appreciation to my family, especially my beloved wife and children. They have not only inspired me but have been my unwavering pillars of support throughout this journey.

This book is also deeply tied to the memory of my mother, who passed away shortly before its publication. As a single, working parent, she embodied the power of faith, love, dedication, and an unyielding resilience that continues to inspire me. Our countless conversations during the writing process were more than discussions about the book; they were cherished moments of connection and profound mutual understanding. Her wisdom, pragmatism, and belief in "just doing it" remain an enduring guide in my life.

Though she is no longer here to see this work completed, I know her spirit lives on in every page, just as she lives on in my heart. This book is as much a reflection of her strength and love as it is of my own efforts. For that, and for so much more, I am and will remain eternally grateful.

To my dear friends, your generosity in offering your time, support, and guidance has been invaluable. You journeyed back in time with me, reliving the fond memories, providing feedback on ideas, and reading the draft chapters. Your involvement has added layers of depth and authenticity to this narrative, and I am forever grateful for your steadfast support.

My exceptional team—Kiki, your constant encouragement, uplifting energy, and invaluable advice have been instrumental in this journey. Andreas, your loyalty, shared passion, and dedication to creating an amazing organization have been inspiring.

To all those who played a role in researching, brainstorming ideas, the editing, and production process, including Leena, Sarah, Caroline, Sara, Scott, and the team at Grammar Factory Publishing. You made these sometimes-daunting tasks feel effortless and enjoyable. Angelika Schultze, your unwavering support for my mother and our family has been a pillar of strength—we are endlessly grateful for all you continue to do.

Lastly, my heartfelt thanks go to my clients and coaches. You are the champions of clarity, consciousness, and compassion, not just in your own lives but also in the lives of your families and organizations. The impact we create together transcends the present moment; it is the foundation we are building for generations to come. Together, we are not only turning houses into loving homes again, but we are also constructing a sturdy foundation upon which future generations can thrive and flourish.

THE DIETRICH
INSTITUTE

A T the Dietrich Institute, we believe that the most powerful kind of success starts at home— with presence, connection, and the courage to lead from the inside out. In a world full of noise and endless striving, we stand for something deeper: love, clarity, leadership, and truth.

We live in a time when burnout is worn like a badge of honor, when homes are quiet and marriages cold, when ambition outpaces connection. The enemy is disconnection—emotional numbness, shallow success, broken relationships, and the chaos of modern life that keeps people stuck in survival mode.

We're here to fight that. Not with platitudes or empty promises, but with a battle-tested approach to reclaiming what matters most. We work with individuals, leaders, entrepreneurs, and community changemakers who are ready to stop drifting and start building lives rooted in truth and love.

This isn't an "enlightening voyage." It's a real, raw, courageous rebuilding—of marriages, families, leadership, and identity. The ripple effect is massive. When one person reconnects with what matters, the impact can transform entire homes, organizations, and communities.

At The Dietrich Institute, we don't do self-help. We do whole-life transformation. Our approach is grounded, evidence-based, and unapologetically relational. We combine expert coaching, deep relationship work, and a powerful community of peers to help you reconnect—to your values, your people, and your purpose.

This is where your house becomes a home. Where marriages get saved. Where leaders show up with heart. Where businesses thrive through emotional alignment and relational strength.

So if you're ready to stop settling for a life that looks good on paper but feels hollow at the core, join us. We're not just building better relationships. We're building a movement—one family, one leader, one home at a time.

Visit www.DietrichInstitute.com/unfogged or follow us on social media to become part of a growing global community that's done playing small.

This is your call to build a life that actually matters.

Relationship Mastery 365

Our flagship program, Relationship Mastery 365, is a twelve-week online course. Initially designed with women in mind, it now reflects the broader philosophy: a high-impact transformation program open to anyone ready to do the deep relationship work.

Relationship Mastery 365 tackles the root cause of most relationship issues: disconnection—not just from your partner, but from yourself, your values, and your inner clarity. It embraces a comprehensive, holistic approach aimed at helping individuals safeguard, strengthen, or save their relationships.

Through expert coaching, evidence-based strategies, and a supportive community, we empower everyone on their relationship journeys, fostering personal growth, enhancing communication, and cultivating lasting intimacy.

This isn't about fixing someone else—it's about reclaiming your own power, presence, and connection.

Don't Let This Be Another Book You Finish and Forget.

If something in these pages hit you—if it cracked something open, if it pissed you off, if it made you feel like you're not crazy after all—good. That's what truth does.

But reading it isn't enough. You've got one life. Don't fog it up. Do something about it . . .

Join the movement

Visit www.DietrichInstitute.com/unfogged

- Get the tools
- Join the tribe
- Start living with fire again

This isn't a self-help funnel. It's a call to arms—for clarity, connection, and real power.

We're not here to balance.
We're here to lead.

ABOUT
THE AUTHOR

CONSTANTIN DIETRICH, known affectionately as Tino, is a dynamic coach, visionary entrepreneur, and an unwavering explorer of the human experience. With an extraordinary journey behind him that spans continents and diverse cultures, Tino now calls the sun-soaked shores of South Florida home, though his path has woven through Germany, Switzerland, Mexico, Canada, the United States, and various other countries across Europe and vibrant Southeast Asia.

Tino's educational quest led him to upstate New York, where he honed his skills and earned a B.Sc. in business administration from Syracuse University, with a focus on international marketing and management. Little did he know that these academic foundations would be the launching pad for his future of innovation and impact.

A sought-after expert on relationships and personal transformation, Tino's insights have been featured in *Rolling Stone*, *Newsweek*, and *Cosmopolitan*. His expertise has also appeared across major television networks, where he offers guidance on navigating relationships in an increasingly complex world. From FOX News to ABC, his appearances have helped millions grasp the importance of clarity and consciousness in building lasting connections.

With deep experience in executive leadership, media, marketing, international business, and consulting, Tino later pursued coaching certification through organizations like Mindvalley and completed executive education at institutions such as the Wharton School. This multifaceted background equipped him to guide individuals, couples, and teams on transformative journeys—drawing from the insights gathered along his global, interdisciplinary path.

Tino's work stands at the frontline of a growing epidemic—disconnection. His mission: to rebuild relationships, restore clarity, and help ambitious people reclaim what truly matters.

After surviving a near-death battle with COVID-19, Tino emerged with a clear conviction: to help others stop sleepwalking through life and start living with radical clarity and connection. His purpose now centers on reducing divorce, healing fractured families, and transforming houses into homes. Over the years, he has seen how this mission touches far more than couples—it ripples out to children, teams, and entire communities.

Throughout his coaching career, Tino has helped couples overcome seemingly insurmountable challenges, rekindle intimacy, and rediscover joy. His work extends beyond romantic relationships, mentoring people worldwide to strengthen their bonds with others—and with themselves.

Through his TRUE method—Tenere, Regnare, Undare, Exaltare—Tino helps clients reclaim inner clarity, reignite drive, and rise with purpose. This is transformation through discipline, self-mastery, and emotional clarity—rooted in courage and built to last.

As founder and CEO of the Dietrich Institute, Tino is a leading voice in personal transformation and compassionate leadership. His entrepreneurial journey spans decades, industries, and cultures. The Dietrich Institute isn't just an institution—it's a call to action. As an independent enterprise and think tank, it offers coaching services that help clients unlock potential, nurture meaningful relationships, and lead with authenticity and purpose.

Tino is also founder and CEO of SNYDER Americas, a disruptive company redefining the multi-billion-dollar golf industry. With precision-engineered, German-designed golf balls, SNYDER delivers unmatched performance and value through a direct-to-consumer model that challenges traditional norms. Over the past years, it has become the official ball of Germany's elite Deutsche Golf Verband and the exclusive ball of the globally recognized Porsche Cup.

Just like his coaching, SNYDER is built on one belief: that true performance doesn't come from tradition—it comes from clarity, courage, and bold reinvention.

By going toe-to-toe with industry giants and delivering premium-quality balls at a fraction of the cost, SNYDER is quickly becoming a household name—embodying bold entrepreneurship and the relentless pursuit of excellence.

For Tino, this work isn't just professional—it's personal. As a husband, father, and survivor, he knows the cost of disconnection and the power of reconnection. Whether coaching couples on the brink, speaking to global audiences, or building the next breakthrough brand, his mission remains the same: to help people reconnect with what—and who—truly matters.

Finding clarity at Clearwater Bay Country Club, Hong Kong.

APPENDIX

Corbinian's Letter to Omi Gila

Corbinian Dietrich
March 22, 2018

Every morning at 6:30, I take our dog out for a walk and make an important phone call. This call is to someone who has helped shape me into the person I am today. Whenever I have a problem or need advice, this person is always there for me. These daily 15-minute conversations are something I look forward to every single day. The guidance I receive has helped me mature and handle situations more effectively. Thanks to this person's advice, I now know how to deal with specific situations better. In fact, it's because of all the guidance I've received that I've grown into the person I am today. The person I'm talking about is none other than my grandmother.

"Don't give up, or you'll never see where it could have taken you." This is one of her favorite sayings, which she tells me often. She has helped me become more determined and taught me to always give my best. Even when things seem to be going downhill, my grandmother is always there to lift me back up. She pushes me to finish what I've started. If I ever come close to giving up on something—something she knows I would regret—she ensures that I don't. Today, I no longer need her to tell me not to give up because I've realized on my own that giving up also means letting go of endless opportunities—opportunities that may

never come again. It's also a waste of all the hard work and effort I've already invested. She has taught me to avoid that.

My grandmother always finds a way to motivate me. She doesn't just make sure I finish my tasks; she also makes sure I feel proud and happy when I do. "Think about your future and look at what I've done in my life. If I had ever given up or stopped motivating myself, you might not even be here today!" This is something she repeats to me over and over again.

She used to be a very successful entrepreneur, and her story of how she achieved her goals inspires me deeply. She once told me about the time she appeared on the cover of a magazine. "I never thought my success would lead to being on the cover of a magazine. But when it happened, I knew that anything is possible!"

"Analyze the situation and always try to see things from the other side's perspective." This might seem like simple advice, but when I was younger and she told me this, it completely changed my outlook. Before, I would quickly get into arguments with my brother, mother, or friends. Now, I try to see things from different perspectives. It has taught me to analyze situations carefully and thoughtfully.

My grandmother is an amazing woman who has helped shape me into the person I am today. I treasure every day I get to spend with her and everything she teaches me.

The 7 Beacons: UNfogged framework

Clarity isn't something you find. It's something you build. These are the beacons that lit the path.

1. **Self-Awareness.** Know who you are. Know what you're not. Own your past, your pain, your patterns. You can't lead a life you don't recognize.

2. **Harmony.** Integrate your ambition with your inner life. Stop swinging between extremes. Discipline and peace don't have to fight each other.

3. **Self-Belief.** Reclaim confidence—not from wins, but from within. The world doesn't give it to you. You were never meant to doubt your fire.

4. **Compassion.** For others. For yourself. Power without compassion is control. You don't need to be soft. You need to be real.

5. **Perspective.** Zoom out. Step back. See what's actually true—not what you've been told to chase. If the ladder's on the wrong wall, who cares how fast you climb?

6. **Purpose.** There's no clarity without direction. Align your life around what matters. Purpose isn't a passion. It's a decision.

7. **Connection.** The final beacon. Without it, everything else crumbles. True power lives in relationships. The goal is never just success. It's intimacy, integrity, and impact.

Next Step: Relationship Mastery 365

If these beacons hit home—good. They were meant to. But reading them is just the beginning.

Relationship Mastery 365 is the next chapter: a high-impact transformation experience built for those ready to:

- Apply this framework to real life
- Master relationships and reignite purpose
- Build a life that doesn't just look good—it feels right

Learn more at
www.DietrichInstitute.com/unfogged

www.ingramcontent.com/pod-product-compliance
Lightning Source LLC
Chambersburg PA
CBHW031457120626
46545CB00005B/1647